SEASONS OF EMOTIONS

Edited by

Joanne Baxter

First published in Great Britain in 2000 by
POETRY NOW
Remus House,
Coltsfoot Drive,
Woodston,
Peterborough, PE2 9JX
Telephone (01733) 898101
Fax (01733) 313524

Copyright Contributors 1999

HB ISBN 0 75430 847 2
SB ISBN 0 75430 848 0

FOREWORD

Although we are a nation of poets we are accused of not reading poetry, or buying poetry books. After many years of listening to the incessant gripes of poetry publishers, I can only assume that the books they publish, in general, are books that most people do not want to read.

Poetry should not be obscure, introverted, and as cryptic as a crossword puzzle: it is the poet's duty to reach out and embrace the world.

The world owes the poet nothing and we should not be expected to dig and delve into a rambling discourse searching for some inner meaning.

The reason we write poetry (and almost all of us do) is because we want to communicate: an ideal; an idea; or a specific feeling. Poetry is as essential in communication, as a letter; a radio; a telephone, and the main criteria for selecting the poems in this anthology is very simple: they communicate.

CONTENTS

THE EXOTIC DANCER

A gracious, stately figure dressed in shades so mellow,
Bright burnished gold and paler shades of yellow,
And as she danced she graciously expressed
The mood the music gave of calm and rest

A change of tempo, and before my eyes
The dancing changed, and much to my surprise
She shed her golden raiment bit by bit,
Shyly at first, but seemingly enjoying it.

Seductively each piece fell to the ground,
And gathered round her feet without a sound,
Louder, the music came, and even faster,
She was the slave, the music was her master.

Crescendo reached - she shook and writhed with pride,
And tossed her filmy garments far and wide,
Oblivious to all who saw her there
She exquisitely disrobed without a care.

The music softened, and her writhing ceased,
She trembled as her modesty increased,
Coquettishly she tried hard to retain
The last small garment, but 'twas all in vain.

And there she stood - cold, nervous but erect,
Her dance accomplished well, without defect,
The wind, her music, had completed her striptease,
She gazed around her neighbours - gaunt, stripped trees.

Lilian Wright

SEASONS OF BEING

Life runs the course of the seasons,
each with a right of its own -
in our maturer years we look back on our youth
and in so many ways can see how we've grown.

Springtime and Easter remind us of birth,
new beginnings, new life ahead
to nourish and nurture, guide and teach
with wisdom right pathways to tread.

Summer encourages energy, zest,
the fullness of life through the years
as development flourishes, aims achieved,
and we learn to deal with our fears.

Falling leaves in their blazing shades
tell their tales of years *edging on,*
missions accomplished (but there's life in the roots),
a few reminiscences of years that have gone.

Winter, it seems, as the season of cold,
implies that these months of the year
signal the end, for life's *given its all* -
but there's fresh life ahead set to cheer.

From start to finish the years roll around,
with chances of freedom and choice.
When we make the most of each season we have,
we can safely *retire* with the echo 'Rejoice!'

Ann Voaden

FALL FLIES IN!

Spring
Never heard Nature's gun
Summer was a non-starter
In a one-horse race
But fall flies in!
Jetting across
Half the continent
Showers of
Blood-orange leaves
Cover New England
Streaming out
To those old Atlantic colonies
Drifting back
Towards skyscraper cities
Where inside elegant apartments
Tête a têtes
Are performed
Over long Manhattans
And sophistication
Rules!

Paul Willkins

REMEMBERED SUFFOLK SUMMER

Kaleidoscopic patterns change and blur
The images of summer. Through the haze
Of fading light remembered pictures stir
The glowing embers of our autumn days.

Morning reveals among the brackish pools
The stilt-legged avocet of bobbing gait,
Scooping with up-curved bill the mollusc jewels,
A regal dish of fare invertebrate;

Or like a chequered arrowhead of light,
A symphony of avian elegance
Taunting the lumbering heron in his flight,
It swoops across the sky in aerial dance.

All nature sleeps beneath the heat of day,
Save for the harrier rising from the fen
To skim wind rippled reed beds for the prey
To carry to his chicks and waiting hen.

Dusk falls to launch the dark winged hawking flight
Above the pallid glow-worms on the heath;
The churring echo of the bird of night.
Beauty from ugliness perceived, beneath.

Now on the shoreline I will walk once more,
Where time worn stones will tell a thousand tales
Of summer and the endless joys it bore,
Land of asparagus and nightingales.

Grahame Godsmark

WINTER WONDERLAND

The snow has arrived, cold and white
hard on the eyes, it's dazzling bright,
falling gently to the ground,
Pristine - making not a sound.
All around looks oh so clean
No scraps of litter can now be seen
It muffles the noise of the traffic roars
Each blade of grass is trimmed with hoar.
The trees' stark branches pierce the sky
to welcome snow from up on high,
For their nakedness a welcome cloak
of glistening white for ash to oak
Children love the snow, it's fantastic
but adults aren't quite so enthusiastic.
Their cars won't start, their steps are slow,
delays occur in the traffic flow.
Although it is a joy to behold
the snow causes problems, manifold.
Yet both children and adults get a thrill
Riding on a sled whizzing down a hill
Their breath hangs on the frosty air, with tobogganing
nothing can compare.
Winter's showcase is open wide and a glittering
Snow Palace is there inside.

M Lister

MOODS

The seasons change and our moods do too
In summer we're happy, but in winter we're blue
The warm summer nights, the hot balmy days
When we're full of the world and enjoy the sun's rays
Then comes the winter, all frosty and cold
When we sit by the fire, feeling so old
The spring gives up hope of the summer to come
Of looking forward to seeing the sun
And autumn with its soft red and brown hues
Trying to prepare us for the wintertime blues
The seasons roll by and our moods move in tune
With the weather around us and all too soon
Our time on this Earth is over and done
And at last with the seasons we now move as one.

Tricia Mackey

FEBRUARY 1993

Old certitudes lost
Flux and age and infirmity
Uncertainty and apprehension

Wind lashes the bushes
Potentilla buddleia cotoneaster
Sparrows shelter in the privet

Perspectives change
Diminishing involvement
As time begets misanthropy

Nicholas Howard

NOVEMBER

When strawberries reappear out of season
When acers put beetroot to shame
When robins sing at early dusk
When all is changed and yet the same.

November with a solemn reputation
November with a mild and softer touch
November when we watch the burning ember
November in the south is just so much.

One day of rain and tempest
One day of blinding sun
One day of silence, fog and mystery
One day of ghosts and fun.

Remember it's the evening of the year
Remember in the month of remembrance
Remember too those no longer here
Remember choruses of hymns and holy chants.

On come the darkest hours and days so short
On come the early morning silver dells
On come autumn's final curtain
On comes a time to listen for the bells.

Denis M Pentlow

OAKS

Loneliness is my
companion
as I stare
into the water's
dull reflection.

The mountains
rise above
the mist,

and in the
clearing,
a carpet of decaying
leaves

sinks back
into the
winter earth,

stroked
by the
twisted
branches
of ancient
oaks
entwined
like lovers.

Michael Lyons

TO THE SEASONS

In wintertime when all is dark and bare
I cuddle up beside the fire.
I hurry home; my work is done.
It's then I look to spring.

In spring when all will come to life
The daffodils I so adore
I feed the hedgehogs and the birds
I take my time in getting home
It's then I look to summer.

In summertime when all has come to life,
The beautiful flowers and trees I admire,
I think of holidays and long fine days,
I enjoy the longest day of the year,
I shudder as I think of autumn.

Autumn is here - and I look back over the year
The trees are shedding their leaves
I hurry home - it's getting cold
And oh! I think of winter.

Winter is here and I say a prayer
I give thanks for many things,
For the bareness of the winter
For the dainty sweetness of spring.
For the trees in full beauty of summer.
For the sun in the sky
And for the beautiful golds and reds of autumn.
And how I look to the seasons.

Janet Cavill

Open Gardens

The season of gardens is upon us
I remember Greenacre so well
The twisting paths and the chill gust
As spring whirlwinds stir the dell.
I remember the fresh leaves budding
The wondrous shades of green,
The sound of the sap almost thudding
As bright spring enlivens the scene.
I remember the slippery pathway
The joy as we turned each bend
And thrilled to the shape of ancient trees
In a garden that has no end.

Hazel Browne

FEBRUARY TULIPS

February tulips, a floral first
A welcome sign not rehearsed
In the wintertimes before
Crocus blooms yet to rise
Pre-daffodils, a big surprise
An overture where sunshine sets the score.

February tulips sing in praise
Of spring to come, of longer days
A taste of living yet to come
They ease the hold of winter's grasp
A sign the cold just will not last
Perhaps to show that spring has nearly sprung

February tulips now abound
Pushing up through winter ground
Blue tits seeking where to make their nest
Winter's giving way to spring
Bumblebees upon the wing
Mother Earth dons a bright new dress

February tulips proudly stand
Cluster here on winter land
A rising birdsong fugue
If winter's done
And spring's to come
The tulips speak of living now renewed

Ray Ryan

SEASONS OF THE SOUL

When doubt and trouble fill my mind and torment ails my soul,
When fears and worries plague my thoughts and billows o'er me roll,
When self and sainthood wage a war and friendless I may be,
When questions, answers, reasons fail and none can set me free,
When prayers are weak and hope seems dim and debts are still unpaid,
When conflict rears its ugly head, self-will and pride pervade.

It's then I need to stop and look, to cast my cares on Him,
To choose His peace, to choose to trust, then patience will begin,
To be content, to give Him thanks, to soar on wings of faith,
To think on all His loveliness, to rest, be still and wait,
To yield, depend, give and forgive, to pray and praise and be . . .
Receive with thanks and then enjoy these gifts He's given me.

And in His time, and His own way, His will be done I know,
As seasons go, this one will pass, His Word has promised so.
And faith would have it be this way, that I may learn the cost
Of love so awesome, so divine, that I would not be lost.
All will be well, His Word is true, my soul will soon be free,
'Trust and obey,' I'll soon be home, His glory I will see.

Teresa D'Ambrosie

YESTERDAYS TOMORROWS

The light began to fade away
As dusk came calling
Birds sang their last songs of day
For morn was now a nightfall away
The night had arrived in full splendour
Dressed in its cloak of black
With polka dot stars shining through
Moths fluttered round street lamps
Street lamps illuminated trees
That swayed to a gentle
Breeze of a summer's night
The dark became light once again
As dawn came calling
Birds sang their first songs of the day
For nightfall was now a morn away.

Kevin Michael Jones

THE LOVELY WHITE SNOW

Silently, fall the whirling flakes of snow
So beautifully white, then dazzling so
Not a sound, not a stir,
Not even a footprint anywhere there
It seems the whole world sleeps
and time will keep
Under this blanket of snow.

Through the window a . . . a Christmas card scene
A lovely white carpet, where the lawn had been
Trees and bushes all dressed in pure white
Now hungry little birds flutter, making dark patches on light
I just gaze and gaze on this glorious winter sight.

Only yesterday, everything was green
Tiny snowdrops and crocus to be seen
Now they have vanished under the snow
But they will come back, as we surely know
with a splash of purple, white and gold, such a pretty show
Bright yellow daffodils will follow on
and soon will be forgotten
the lovely, white snow.

Edna Parrington

CHRISTMAS

Christmas time is here again
With all goodwill and cheer;
The snow lies on the hedgerows
And a robin chirps quite near.

The lakes are cold and frozen,
The ducklings slide around,
The air is crisp and very cold,
And frost is on the ground.

Holly trees are full of berries,
With large thick clusters red,
All waiting for the birds to come -
It's wonderful how they're fed.

We love to come into our home
Where the air is warm and sweet.
By the flames of heat at chimney breast
We like to warm our hands and feet.

Our house is freshly decorated
With holly and tinsel galore:
The Christmas tree stands tall and high
With wrapped gifts both big and small.

When evening shadows slowly gather
We hear a sound so sweet outside -
The pleasant singing of a carol
Wishing us goodwill and joy.

'Joy to the world, the Lord has come,
Let Heaven receive Her King'
The baby Jesus in cattle stall lies
Because there was *no room* in the inn.

They all sang again with a question for all:
Have *you* any room for Jesus, God's son?
He has come that you might go free,
He died for *you,* which includes everyone.

The carol singers went on their way
With their lanterns shining bright,
And we indoors were joyous and gay
Because the Saviour was born on that starry dark night.

Violet Impey

THE SEASON IN QUESTION

Winter is here, manifest without a doubt,
Branches are leafless coated in crisp moss
The cold wind stirs and scatters
Myriads of floating ice petals, silently,
Softly, falling to gloss -
The earth sharp with stiletto grass blades
Crunching as footsteps tread their way to
Collect logs that will imitate summer as
They spit in a hearth, crimson and gay.

Winter is here for this life of mine
Spring, summer and autumn has been
Delighted in time and time again.
Yet why do I feel another spring is so near?
Like the buds on the branches just waiting to appear
As a clarion call cutting through snow
New life is around the corner,
Soft breezes will blow
Snowdrops and primroses waiting to break through
Blossom to cascade, limbs to be pliant,
Emotions to woo,
Coated by the future as it drowsily waits
Embracing chilled winter and walking through spring's gates.

Joan Richardson

SUMMER'S SUBURBAN GARDEN

From where I sit with tired stare
three swifts play games in open air
a high pitched song that lasts not long
fades away for ever.

While on the ground and well renowned
for chanting in the night
a mass of frogs call out like dogs; far
but out of sight

Colours dim to shades of grey
which bring a cool dusk breeze
the light from home begins to roam
like moonlight on the trees

Hordes of moths both small and large
create a glistening sky
as stars appear that twinkle dear
like echoes from on high

Darkened views and stunted sounds
begin to fade away
for nature takes a different course
until another day . . .

Andy Rosser

THE SHELL SHOP - KEWSTOKE 1999

There is a tempting fascinating place we like to go
Where heavy rose quartz cups hold candles' glow
This veritable Aladdin's cave long ago we found
And wood chimes overhead make a charming tinkling sound
Semi-precious gems artfully wink their charms of every kind
Enchanting concepts call to one and draw the mind
Curiosities everywhere tucked away in nooks
Floral-decked bric-a-brac, lucky beans, tea towels, cards and books

Like sleeping beauties resting behind protective glass
Are gleaming precious shells, sea coral in a special class
Perhaps the best, a massive twinkling amethyst geode
But equally bewitching affordable delights for childish hands to hold
This is where we cheer ourselves when life seems dull or full of woe
This fascinating tempting place is where we like to go
But now the days close in with winter drawing near
Temptations of the crystal cave must wait until next year

Shirley Flower

EBB AND FLOW

The seasons come,
And the seasons go,
The seasons ebb,
And the seasons flow.

The spring green hue,
The rich autumn gold,
The clear summer blue,
The grey winter cold.

The changing mask
Of our Mother Earth,
Winter her death,
And spring her rebirth.

Spring starts the tune,
Autumn beats the time,
Summer sings the song,
Winter blows the chime.

The seasons change,
Yet all stay the same,
Nature's illusion;
Her own magic game!

The seasons come,
And the seasons go,
The seasons ebb,
And the seasons flow . . .

Clive Blake

Once A Year

Have you seen the carpet
That falls down from the trees
Full of wonderful colours
That you've ever seen?

So lovely to walk on
It can cover your boots
You can kick it, and throw it
And not care two hoots

This carpet is magic
Comes just once a year
The pile is so special
This one doesn't wear

All children love it
It's heaven to them
It crackles when jumped on
Again and again

They can't make it dirty
Their fun is just great
With these sweet autumn leaves
That come rather late

Now this special carpet
Is there for us all
Just allowed once a year
In the time called *The Fall.*

Joyce West

A SEASON'S KISS

With each and ev'ry passing day, I find
The shadow of the hour hand begin
To lengthen, as the sun returns to wind
The season's clock to welcome in the spring;
And daffodils, with golden trumpets, sound
The anthem of the coming season, where
New life begins and pleasant days are found
Enriched by nature's priceless solitaire;
And marvel I, as such a wondrous sight
Unfolds before my very eyes, and rays
Of sunlight capture God's creative might,
Revealing promises of summer days:
How beautiful this blessed season is,
When life is all transformed by nature's kiss.

Graeme Leslie Jennens

THE SEASON OF CONTRAST

The pure white snow scurries around,
Landing gently on the ground
Silently carpeting, glistening white,
Under the darkness, a wintry sight.
No wind, no noise, a silence so strange.
A backdrop of snow, scenery to change.
White is above you, beside you and down
Silence is golden, this night there's no sound.

Outside is white, cold and serene
The world is asleep, no one is seen.
In contrast a different picture is met,
Fires are lit as winter does set.
Burning embers, crackling, bright,
Warming now after the crisp, cold night.
Hot mulled wine on the fireplace.
Heart-warming for all, a saving grace.

Christmas lights twinkle on the tree.
Children's laughter, full of glee.
Pleased to dress and rush outside,
In the snow to play and hide.
The smell of cooking wafts around,
Music plays a happy sound.
Winter's a season to cherish each year,
Especially Christmas with all its good cheer.

Carol Bubb

MR ROBIN - ALL IN FUN

Hopping along the hedge so green
With no idea where he's been
But where he's going, he knows best
He is the little robin redbreast.

He comes to tell us winter's here
With frosty mornings bright and clear
A warning siren on his chest
He is the robin redbreast.

If you put out some nuts and treats
He'll remember where he eats
And come back every year, I bet
To show off his bright red robin's breast.

Suie Nettle

NATURE COULD MAKE A MISTAKE

Amidst shouts of despair, my curiosities wandered
Up above with clouds hand in hand.

Some of them just dropped out like a flash in the air.
A few remained to roam about in my desert of thirsty sand.

My curiosity urged me to a big jump off the ground,
Space and the planet to explore, on new Mars to land.

This curiosity of mankind is a real ultimatum to the nature
Man to be the master of universe seems not out of hand.

Curiosity is a mysterious gift of nature to mankind.
Nature could make a mistake, I cannot understand.

M Yaqub Mirza

SILLY OLD FOOL

A winter morning's sunshine glows bright across the land
children dress in hats and coats, to school go hand in hand.

Faces red and hearts aglow they skip along, no cares or woe.
Where are those days for me now? Where have the years flown?
For now my winter mornings seem dark and dull, I moan.

Well I think it's time to take a day to become a child again
breaking ice upon the puddles and playing in the rain
not bothered if I get wet, not bothered if I'm cold
my heart tells me to do this but my body says too old.

So I sit and watch the children on the way to school
and tell myself to cheer up you silly old fool . . .

Shaun Gilbertson

A Fallen Leaf - From That Time Of Year!

Walking across
wide open fields,
my gift of sight
is drawn to a fallen leaf
with colours,
red, brown, green
 and rich yellow, gold.
Now holding
that fallen leaf
in the palm of my hand,
thoughts come into mind,
not the works
of fallen man,
it is the work
of Nature's art.
It is the thoughts of creation's ways
at work,
without a doubt
adding her beauty
to our globe.
I am held spellbound
by the changing colours
seen on the full- grown trees
adding their own beauty
to the world of man.
If I was asked,
'Tell me
what's impressed you
this very day of life?'
I would have to be honest
in my reply
from my very living soul.

A leaf
fallen from a tree,
with colours
that delight,
my gift
of sight
is this silent wonder
I have seen
as I was blessed
when walking often over fields
with soft earth
under my feet.
Now, at this changing time
of the year
it seems to offer
a total peace
to our very busy world
and ways of life
that, in itself,
finds no time to stop,
then gaze
at all the silent wonders
before the eyes.

                    Amen.

R P Scannell

WHAT SEASON'S BEST?

Creatures wake up from a cosy sleep
Spring flowers appear for their first peek
In fields all around lambs are born
Nights get lighter sun is warm.

Bunnies hop and March hares run
Rolling Easter eggs, such fun
Birds sing, dew, grass starts to grow
I never want the spring to go.

A walk in the country on a summer's day
The smell of cut grass and fresh cut hay
Busy bees and butterflies, some of them rare
Warm breeze blowing through my hair
Picking buttercups and making daisy chains
Gathering brambles in country lanes
Cows with their newborn happy grazing
The summer season is just amazing.

Burnt oranges and browns we start to wear
To match leaves falling everywhere
We think of squirrels collecting food
Climb trees for chestnuts in the wood
Toffee apples, trick or treat
Autumn is very hard to beat.

I love to wake up on a winter's day
It is frosty and snowing all the way
A bowl of hot porridge and away you go
Snowballs pelting to and fro.

Log fires burning, chimneys reek
All bring roses to my cheeks
Christmas cake and ginger wine
Winter is my favourite time.

Rosemary Gladwell

AUTUMN

The months of the year come fluttering down,
In colours of red yellow orange and brown,
Aimlessly, gracefully, making no sound,
Caught by the wind - up down and around.
Lost friendships, bereavement, frustrations of life,
Redundancy, quarrels and neighbourly strife.
All these become memory as days pass on by,
Soon new leaves will bud 'neath a bright warm spring sky,
So farewell to bad times, sad memories and more,
Let us kick the dead leaves as they cover the floor,
We look forward to new months whatever they hold,
With new friendships and interests, opportunities of gold.
If we learn from the past it is hoped we will see,
Dead thoughts float away like autumn leaves from a tree.

Anita E Matthews

AUTUMN JEWELS

Blankets of mist shroud the landscape,
There's a spiky chill in the air,
A silence prevails,
Whilst the trees patiently await
The glow of the morning sun.

The mystical beauty of nature awakens,
Dewdrops trickle in silvery threads,
The fiery aura
Of ruby red brambles, hawthorn, hips,
Mingling 'neath an ice blue sky.

Fluffy seed-heads, bronzed bracken in the sun,
Rustling leaves dancing in the breeze,
A dreamlike wonder
Of majestic oaks, splashed in colourful splendour,
Remembrance of a glorious autumn day.

Diana Frewin

LAND OF MY BIRTH

England fair country of my birth,
Created by God when he fashioned the earth.
Flowers nurtured with loving care,
Bloom in colourful array everywhere.

Fast flowing rivers, rippling streams,
Shimmering reflections and time for daydreams.
Those happy days that swiftly pass,
With sounds of lawnmowers cutting the grass.

Pebble beaches, bright golden sand,
White cliffs and rocky shores, shape our fair land.
Fields now golden with ripened corn,
Harvested one glorious September morn.

Now summer turns to autumn time,
Colours of trees are truly sublime.
Daylight lessens, as the weeks pass,
Diamond-like dewdrops glisten on the grass.

Lightning flashes, thundery rain,
Lashing furiously against the windowpane,
Leaves in profusion on the ground,
In strong winter gales are blowing around.

Flurries of snow begin to fall,
And look pretty on the high garden wall.
Snow falls steadily through the night,
Covering green fields with carpets of white.

Icy patches on the highway,
Those tedious journeys on the railway.
New growth heralds the birth of spring,
And in the hedgerows birds begin to sing.

Of all the places on this Earth,
I thank God for England, land of my birth.

Doreen M Bowers

AUTUMN

I feel the summer heat recede,
I sense the countryside is freed,
I hear the rustle of the leaves,
October swirling in the eaves,
Once more the feisty pheasants lurk,
The village school is back at work,
I see again across the leas
The slender shimmering Suffolk trees,
The bonfire pile begins to rise,
I sigh at sunsets in the skies,
The hymns are sung, the harvest's past,
The Waveney flows mighty fast,
Adorned in gold again you came,
A thousand thousand years the same,
Yet always different, always new,
Oh autumn, how I cherish you!

Peter Davies

FALLING LEAVES

Autumn now the leaves are falling
We surely hear the Saviour calling
'Ye who are weary follow me
And your salvation I will be'

Red, gold and brown
The leaves come down,
With their beauty
One alone from realms above
Will bless this season with His love.

How I love the falling leaves,
And sometimes see the golden sheaves,
Now harvest home is all our song
And echoing in the twilight long
We chant our praises to our King
For all the mercies He dost bring.

Marcella Pellow

WINTER IS HERE

I wake in the morning and all that I see,
Is a cold and wet day waiting for me,
Umbrella's are up and the coats are on,
We can finally say the summer has gone.

People are rushing to get out of the rain,
Many are catching the bus or train,
In the summer most people will walk to work,
Just wearing some trousers along with a shirt.

The winter is here and has finally set in,
Put on a brave face for whatever it brings,
It may be a bad winter, that I do not know,
But whatever it is, to work we must go.

When the snow starts to fall the ground is white,
It can take a long time to clear out of sight,
The roads can be dangerous when there is ice,
So before you speed - you'd better think twice.

P Daly

SEPTEMBER

Autumn or fall
Enrich our gardens
With fallen leaves in warm colours
Red, orange and burnt brown.
The orange sky
At the end of the day
Completes the warm array
Grassy paths
And cyclamen
White, pink
Add to the colourful garden
On a September day
Amaryllis belladonna
With its pink petals and
White starry throated blooms
Prosper against a sunny spot.

J M Stoles

THOUGHTS

The countryside is calming green with nature's beauteous things,
With all the gold of paradise borne on summer's wings.
Fledglings soaring bravely sing with new-found joy,
Competing with the snoring of a lazy, farmer's boy.
We look at seas of ripening corn and burning strips of sand,
Whilst watching lovers strolling through the twilight hand in hand.
And then the lengthening shadows bring summer to a close,
And we talk of lazy holidays and sun in retropose;
Living gladly on the memory of the days just passed away,
Whilst waiting for sunlight of another summer's day.

But then it's Indian summers and we saunter through the town,
In golden shades of autumn, and leaves of russet brown,
Those rimy fingers cold and thin go creeping through the night
Painting icy pictures, a startling virgin white.
Autumn shades are fallen leaving carpets warm and deep,
Of rotting leaves now swirling out beneath our booted feet.
The wind is cutting keenly as it blows in from the East,
And we think of tea and crumpets as we hasten to the feast.
Then peeping through the curtains the sun glows coldly red;
We turn and snuggle warmly in the comfort of our bed.

We walk in winter slowly with our faces cold and numb,
Our thoughts now turning springward to nature's ripening plum.
We talk with breath so icy sharp we almost feel the pain,
Whilst longing in our frozen hearts for April's warming rain.
But there is joy in living when the snow is crisp and white,
With children shrilly playing - abandoned with delight;
In making rolling snowballs as they hurtle down the hill,
And follow in toboggans excited when they spill.
We shout in winter gladly and praise the Holy Son,
As our thoughts move to the future and the miracles to come.

Corrie Francis

WINTER SKY

Oh how I utterly detest the winter sky
Its dreary expectations make me sigh
The clouds look like a pale grey stain
Might we once again expect some rain?
The trees are shivering in the breeze
I pray for summer down on my knees
There is no life nothing laughs or sings
Oh give me the warmth sunshine brings
It's as if the world is in slow motion
Affected by some deadly potion
The hours sit heavy, my mind's a mess
Now even the clock seems motionless
I need a different point of view
Someone to remind me dark days are few
I know children can, they are the very light
When they dance and play and scream and fight
Suddenly there, in the sky, what a lovely shade of blue
It's filling up my senses, with warmth and hopes anew
Yes I know the earth is sleeping I know it must be done
I can't help the way I feel without my friend the sun
But I'll see my kids tonight they are my rays of light
And their beautiful sweet faces will help me win my fight

Michael Bellerby

OF BOTH SEASONS - AN ANALOGY

Nature's yearly seasons approach like age
stealthily as a cat with growing rapidity
from spring to summer, autumn then winter,
childhood spring fresh in joy and laughter blooms
till reaches the age of delicate sixteen,
horizons expand, ideas cement until 21!
Summer arrives, takes over till sunset
at the age of 65, the autumn of our lives:
'tis sad to relate winter's undefined date
when man with nature are joined in one!

Howard Thorn

MY MOORLANDS

Walking on my moorlands
Is where I love to be
My thoughts run deep and silent
the quiet vastness all around
No crowds no noise of people
Only nature's sounds
Ponies wild roam free
Peace is all about
Hooves stamping upon the ground
Foxgloves tall and proud
Sway to and fro
Heather's purple and white as
Far as my eyes can see
Ferns and wild flowers
Shelter from the moor's winds
A sense of feeling lost in time
In another time far far away
You wonder is it here to stay?
Clouds swirl around the vast sky
A breeze does gently blow
For summer's here at last
To stay never wanting to go
Taking in deep breaths
The air is sweet and fresh
Many paths lead far and wide
Each one gives out a feeling
Of time where many travelled before
No doors to shut behind me
Only windows open wide
It's wonder after wonder
My moorland countryside.

Valerie Anderson

AUTUMN FALLS

Autumn sits in his throne room,
Adorned by robes of red and brown,
He waits for winter to take his place
The trees as his courtiers, their leaves as his crown

With the age of the oak on his shoulders,
And the wisdom of beasts in his heart,
The knowledge of death starts to haunt him;
A vision of life torn apart

He knows what it is to be hunted
And he flees, though it wearies him much
Until, almost frozen with sadness,
He surrenders to winter's chill touch

Laurence Winder

WINTER GARDEN

Outside, late January's mourning grey
enshrouds the snow-pied garden, now forlorn,
and nature's embryonic life sleeps deep
around the speckled, slow-surrendering lawn.
No feather-flutter in the barren bush
disturbs the torpid tenor of the scene.
The strange monastic silence seems to await
cowled figures where lately the flowers have been.
Defiantly, the willow and the ash,
their fallen finery around their feet,
flaunt an immodest nakedness in death,
raising bare limbs. Vainglorious conceit!
But, flaring against the crumbling, grey stone wall
cotoneaster's vibrant berries give
promise of lusty life and vigour still,
rivalling the kingly holly's will to live.

Soon snowdrops, happy heralds of the spring
will once again start bravely burgeoning.

Patricia Healey

THE SPRING PARADE

Fresh and lush the green shoots stretch
And reach towards the sun.
Spring is looming, glistening light,
Dark, dead winter's almost done.

Purple velvet splashed with yellow,
Beautiful perfection.
A dainty iris standing proud
Saluting Earth's conception.

Next the snowdrops burst with life
Parasols of white and lime,
Crocuses and daffs and tulips
March along to the rhythm of time.

A blanket of ivy against the wall
Gives backdrop to myriad shades
Painted, dotted on the green
Welcome the Spring Parade!

Janet Williams

MAY DAY

Heady the scent of the May
The lark's song heralds the day.
Soft shimmers the grass with morning dew
The buttercup shows her face to the sun.
Shall I hold one beneath your chin
to see if you like butter?
Will I a daisy chain make for you
and hang it around your neck?
Mayhap upon your cheek
place a loving peck;
or ask the primrose to gild you a crown of gold.
Let me gather the lady-smock
to make you a small nosegay
for I have chosen you my love to be my
Queen of the May.

Avis E Wolfenden

WINTER DAYS

The garden gate is swinging
On its hinges in the wind
The weather's getting colder
Seems the winter now begins
The countryside will change its face
With trees now almost bare
Different shades of green and brown
Appearing everywhere
The crisp cold winter days
Still bring a magic to our world
With frost to cover all
When we awake as day unfurls
And with the fall of evening
Moon and stars will light the night
Casting shadows here and there
Adds mystery to our flight
The warmth and comfort
We all seek
Is there when we reach home
For winter has so much to share
Enjoy each day to come

Jeannette Gaffney

MY ENGLAND

Oh wonderful England
Oh country of mine
How you astound me
With beauty divine

Of all that you are
And of all that you be
I'll treasure fore ever
My time upon thee

I'll relish each morning
When first I arise
The sight I receive
Through my wondering eyes

Resplendently rising
Thou glittering sun
In silence descending
When daylight is done

Whether crispy white snow
Or fresh sparkling rain
Thy beauty outshineth
Again and again

No reason for roaming
or searching for wonder
For beauty lies waiting
Just way out yonder

Susan Kitchen

AUTUMN

Suddenly, it's autumn.

Only yesterday, loving a lingering summer warmth,
    Autumn still seemed far away:
        The garden was full of colour,
        The grass was dry and sweet to walk on,
        The air was mild.

But today, the wind is cold and rough,
    Rain is beating against the windowpanes.
        Everything is drenched,
        There is a carpet of leaves under the trees,
        The sky is dark.

For a moment my heart sinks.

But then I remember:
    Autumn means fires,
           golden leaves,
           spiders' webs shining with dew,
           chestnuts,
           blackberries,
    and best of all, preparations for Christmas -
        that loveliest time of the year!

Father, help me to be content
And to find Your beauty in every season.

Margaret Dawson

WINTER PATH

Old and bare are the trees
In the winter wood.
Still and frosty and cold
As they ever stood.

Not a leaf nor a twig will stir
In the icy air,
Not a sound in the stony silence.
Not a bird there.

But down 'neath the frozen grass
And the leaf-piled wall,
Creatures are deeply sleeping
Safe from it all.

In the evergreen hedges
Where the leaves cling
Robin and wren may be hiding,
Head beneath frozen wing.

Beneath hard clods of earth
Bluebells are asleep.
Their burgeoning undisturbed
Where they lie deep.

No distressing sound will break
Their winter's rest
Until the coming of spring
Calls them in beauty dressed.

Mary Johnson-Riley

WINTER'S HERE

Piercing chill wind comes to call,
Deathly child of autumn's fall,
Ghostly face with frozen stare,
Crisp coverlet of blinding glare.

Holding flesh within its grip,
Freezing nose and numbing lip,
Strips the trees and leaves them bare,
Blanches eyebrows, cheeks and hair.

Hexagons of frosted lace,
Floating down to Earth from space,
Flakes from heaven gently shower,
And death holds life in dormant power.

Icicles like daggers drawn,
Swords which cut the cold, grey dawn,
Poised and hanging from the eaves,
Dripping on the crusted leaves.

Squirrels leap with athletes' ease,
Flicking brush through frosty trees,
Skaters skim the mirror pond,
While sun sets wearily beyond.

Vixen in her hidden lair,
Resplendent with her chestnut hair,
In her burrow, gone to ground,
Cowering from huntsman's hound.

Robin, with his vest of red,
Picking worms from farmer's tread,
Dark skies shedding frozen tears,
telling us that winter's here.

Jennifer D Wootton

THE SEASONS

The sun is shining bright today
And all the clouds have rolled away
The children have their raincoats scorned
They're outside playing where it's warm.
The bees are humming near the flowers
The air is sweet from April showers
Winter's gone. It's lost its prime
Spring is now. Then Summertime.
Holidays and picnics too
Seas are green and skies are blue
Children playing in the sand
Farmers ploughing up their land.
Then comes straw and silage making
Bales of hay and all the rakings
Autumn's here: the leaves are falling
Can you hear that Winter's calling?
So here we are back to square one
The seasons come and then they're gone
And so the Winter's nearly done
We wait again for Spring to come.

Virginia Barrasin

AUTUMN IS HERE

Autumn is here;
Now woodlands take on auburn tints,
Mists linger - intangible, ethereal;
The glinting sun has lost its might.

A swirl of bonfire smoke drifts
Through the murky outlines of trees,
Now brittle-boned and crisped by frost.
Somewhere, something scuttles in the gloom.

Orchards unleash their ripened treasures,
Russet and golden, tumbled on the dying ground;
The smell of wood smoke mingles
With damp earth and forgotten, shrivelled apples.

Whirling winds hurl copper-crested leaves
To the leaden skies
Where swallows huddle on lone telegraph wires,
Then flee, heralding the arrival of winter.

Vikki Silverlock

SEASONS PASSING

The peaceful sound of summer
Passing
As I hear birds in full flight
Passing
Heightens to the full my life in
Passing
This peaceful sound of summer

The dying sound of autumn
Passing
As stately trees turn gold in
Passing
Mourns the death of each summer
Passing
This dying sound of autumn

The silent sound of winter
Passing
As cushioned floors of snowflakes
Passing
Turn darkened beds to white in
Passing
Sleep soundly now for time is
Passing
This silent sound of winter.

The living sound of springtime
Passing
As joyful scenes of new birth
Passing
Hope for all as we see them
Passing
This living sound of springtime

Michael Widdop

AUTUMN THRENODY

A sad time
when summer slips away
and the equator-seeking sun
withdraws its golden gifts
as the chilly autumn days
serve us notice that
the hard relentless
grip of winter
is now upon its way.

Dark clouds of swallows
chatter as they gather
mustering for their weary trip
following the guiding sun
upon their long, long journey south.

Now autumn paints its colours
upon the submissive land
as the leaves turn from green
to brown, red, russet and yellow
as they flutter like
tinted snowflakes down
to the sleeping Earth . . .

Stephen Gyles

THE RIA FORMOSA GALLOPING TOWARDS WINTER

Sandy hillocks surround my mood,
tufted with faded grey-blonde grasses,
like ageing human hair.

Kernel clean, dead brown spikes of sea holly,
once turquoise and amethyst,
blow their thorny leaves, now transparent and torn,
across the beach, waiting to stab
The bare-footed walker.

Wizened stalks of wheat stubble and old abandoned
corn cobs, mouldering into the grave of the earth,
flow into silver flecked dune vegetation.
The once glossy feathers fried to brittleness,
like the muzzle of an aged mongrel bitch.

Parched barley husk fields and limed bone beech-wood
are nature's decaying remnants defeated by their efforts
to seed and regenerate.

The echo of rising sap, fresh spongy bark,
and the sweet young perfume of the orange blossom,
sadden me, adding to my reverie,
a sense of death,
of something dying.

Patricia Lynwood

AS THE LEAVES BEGIN TO FALL

The spring showers and the warming sun
The rising sap and the newborn green
Are now but treasured memories
As the leaves begin to fall.

The rich, throbbing days of summer
With their vibrant fruitfulness
Are yesterday's joys
As the leaves begin to fall.

Yet clothed in autumn splendour -
Reds and gold and burnished browns -
Their beauty is unsurpassed,
As the leaves begin to fall.

O Lord, grant us grace, that we may now
Prepare ourselves for winter snow
As the leaves begin to fall.

Gerallt

WINTER, WAITING FOR SPRING

Winter, snows, white covered roads
the robin in the garden sits on a spade handle
as through the window comes a soft light
delicate as any candle
While the robin chirps for his mate
the cat sits high upon the gate
knowing that this meal will not be his
he's just looking!
An old dog, of undetermined breed,
sits forlorn
Too lazy to move,
looking forward to breakfast
and a warm fire,
Not that his need is dire,
his kennel is quite warm,
warm enough for a mild storm,
proof against the snow
although he may not seem to know
it's there he should go
for his own sweet comfort
The cock of the roost comes out to greet the day
in his own particular way
as the farmer's wife starts to say
it is time to get out of the hay.
'I'll start the breakfast,' says her spouse
and the rattle of the pans
hitting the oven burners
panics a tiny mouse.

A J Marchant

LATE AUTUMN

Each fallen leaf, once vital,
A living thing - no more,
Creates a bed so soft
For raindrops that cascade,
From clouds as black as night,
Reflecting like small mirrors
In the autumn sunshine,
That accompanies the vivid blue sky,
Wispy clouds, that herald
Storms at sea, with the seagulls
Seeking refuge from gale force
Winds and lashing rain,
Stinging like a thousand insects
In the faces of those
That challenge the elements
To prove - no submission.
Now in the forest, trees tall,
Stark, waiting for the spring
To bring new life, as
Nature never fails,
Where woodland creatures prepare
To sleep through winter's spell
With berries, nuts - hidden stores,
To help survive the coming season!

T G Bloodworth

SEASONS

As the autumn leaves blow across the ground:
The wind gets up and they go whirling around,
rapidly turning them into confusion,
Their beautiful colours create an illusion.

Vividness of colouring all shades and sizes,
Red, green, yellow, orange and some surprises.
How can one say God did not make a tree?
When he gave us such beauty, and for free.

Each season as it comes and goes,
Such variety, in winter we get snow.
It sparkles and glitters, like a twinkling star,
When trying to go to work, you could see it far.

In spring we get all the fresh green leaves,
We can smell the freshness when we breathe.
It's amazing how from death comes life,
Like a new baby from a loving wife.

It rejuvenates the family,
Brings you together, when two become three.
God is still working miracles, now in our age,
There is no explanation, I know at this stage.

But all you have to do is look at nature's ways,
The summer brings flowers, and bright sunny days.
We should be thankful, to our Lord above,
For sending such verity, all with his love.

Sylvia M Harbert

LONG YEARS AGO, THAT SPRING

How new green the leaves did flutter in the breeze
That late October morning I did believe it spring.
Light, sky, Renoir colours richly sparkling on the lawn,
And cool breathy sweetness on the blushed blue air
That brushed my skin like the soft lips of a baby's kiss
Told me it was spring, powdered in hope and promise.
Butter yellow light darting kite-like through the trees
Gleamed with tenderness in supple youth not age as
Then within that autumn spring I walked across a green
And my heart skipped a beat and broke as I looked out
And saw an old love's smiling vision waiting in the place,
That self-same place, where she in quiet had stood when
I declared my love to her long years ago, that spring.
I halted in wonder that some wistful image deep inside
Forgetting had risen up and interposed itself between
My seeing and its light as completed image of a kind
Raised up, projected outward, from vision going blind.
Now quiet came upon me as I reached to take her hand
Outstretched and saw her smile up close so broad and
Grand and heard her voice as musical, all resonant
In concert with the questioned amusement consonant
With those brown eyes as they always did look up at me
And I spoke, fully smiled hello, let go and walked away
As once she moved on forward, left me motionless that day.
O, man and earth and love are all alike in things they share
Nor can they forfeit justice they're allotted, not one season,
Though time cannot turn back again, whatever wish or reason;
Yet, fall's illusion reached across suspended youth to bring
A final path for man and earth and love, to walk on, even sing,
And never stop to look back once, long years ago, that spring.

Edgar Wyatt Stephens

SEASONS OF CHANGE

It clears the splinters,
For the birth of a new year.
Fragments of light-glass balance,
Upon threads of an abandoned web.
Lost lambs dance merrily in blue haze.

As the cart wheel turns on,
Sunbeams bright on burning backs.
Heat blisters burst on baby toes.
Heatwaves crash
On sunshine junkies.
Feeding on a needle of hay,
An elderly farmer drifts away.
In a pathetic porthole of the peace.
The whispering waterfront wheels and rolls,
In his blackened corner.

Night chills hear
Rustlings of paper-bag trees.
Parcels of light-leaf chevy,
In hurried breeze.
They scatter sensitive, shy, shuddering.
On the swamp green landscape,
Cows lie down.
Prepared.

Midnight strikes,
Daggers, polished.
Stand firm through pipes.
Soldiers. In line to face battle,
Clearing the splinters for the birth of a new year.

Lisa Andrews

SUMMER

It's summertime in England, there's a magic in the air
As nature in full glory shows her beauty everywhere.
Gardens filled with roses, glistening with morning dew
Create pictures of perfection with their various shades of hue
Whilst in the meadows, like clusters of spun gold.
Beneath the sun buttercups their petalled head unfold
Keeping them company, so modest and so small
Grow petal-eyed daisies, the prettiest of them all
There amongst the hedgerows, the wild flowers spread
Creating as much beauty as any cultivated bed.
The butterflies and bees as they flit along their way
Give the added perfection to every summer's day.
Summer also mean picnics and outdoor fun.
Lazy days and holidays, relaxing in the sun,
Visiting the country or enjoying the seaside air.
Yes, summer in old England is quite beyond compare
But summer doesn't always mean skies of azure blue.
For God's growing creations, need refreshing rain too
It's this combination that makes England oh so green
And helps create beautifully the perfect summer scene.

Audrey Harrison Rimmer

THE SEASONS

Winter, oh, so beautiful!
With frost upon the ground
Glistening like icing
Leaves newly crowned

Nipping toes and fingers
Painting noses red
Breath like a heavy mist
Cheeks feeling dead

But spring brings hope anew
Buds poking through for sun
God's way of showing new birth
All dead nature gone

A vast array of colour
Like the rainbow coloured bright
A promise of good things to come
Giving hope and faith and light

Summer in all its glory
Bright sunshine cheers our lives
Sandy beaches, holidays
Long leisurely drives

Trees dressed up with blossom
Standing tall and straight
Apple blossom forming velvet paths
All this God did create

Autumn gives us time to rest
Preparing for Christmas praise
Autumn is a dying time
Christmas our hopes will raise
Hope in a child so small
Bringing peace to one and all.

Alma Taylor

MY FAVOURITE SEASON

I love the summer, the warmth and the sunshine the scent of
new-mown hay.
Warm breezes rustling through feathery green leaves, filtering the
sun's hot rays.
Roses and honeysuckle climb in profusion, heady perfume fills the air.
Sounds of music and happy laughter from a distant village fair.
Children paddle in foam-spumed water breaking on shifting
golden sand.
While crowds relax on bright coloured deckchairs listening to lively
promenade bands.
Tea on the lawn - cricket on the green.
Who could ask for a more peaceful summer scene?

Autumn also weaves its magic, green fields give way to golds
and browns.
Misty mornings moist with dewdrops - mushrooms on the ground
The breeze is now not quite so gentle as it snatches at the trees.
They lose their battle, release their offspring to fall and flutter -
fancy free.
Harvest is gathered in each little hamlet - people sing their praises for
the bounteous gifts that our God has given and these beautiful
golden days.
Bonfires and fireworks and Hallowe'en.
Autumn departs like a stately queen.

Winter now is fast approaching - the frosts make our feet and
fingers glow.
Soon the fields and woodlands will lie silent under a carpet of dazzling
white snow.
Down by the marshes the curlew are calling, their plaintive notes fall on
crisp clear air.
The fox runs the gauntlet of hounds and horses - seeking the safety of
his lair.
Holly berries and ivy festoon the hedgerows - fir trees are waiting their
turn to be chosen to glitter with tinsel and baubles while the log fires
brightly burn.
Robins so perky - mince pies and turkey.
Winter is truly a wonderland.

Soon festivities of Christmas are left behind us - we can start to think
of Spring.
Of hopes and plans and new beginnings that only a new year can bring.
Buds burst forth on trees and flowers - the world is green again.
Primroses, daffodils, bluebells and violets are kissed by the gentle rain.
Baby lambs gambol - birds nest in the hedgerows - skylark sings high in
the skies.
Meadows exchange their drab cloaks for a mantel of multicoloured
flowers and butterflies.
April showers. balmy breezes, the elusive cuckoo's call.
There are countless more reasons why spring is my season.
The most beautiful season of all.

Elsie Francis

SUMMER: THE ENCHANTMENT OF TWILIGHT

Dusk, that time of night,
When trees, etched black against the failing light
Catch the last glimmers of the fading day
And wait for stars, their twinkling tune to play.
The sky takes on a different hue,
Lighter pinks merging with a deeper blue,
Where fluttering martins greet with a peep,
Catching the last moth, err they sleep,
Await the entrance of the hooting owl.

Fragile clouds come sailing by,
Flirting with the changing sky
Like nubile maidens in diaphanous white
Show just enough to quicken sight,
Meet and kiss and fade away,
Reborn anew at break of day,
Floating on the fleeting tide,
Await the entrance of the hooting owl.

David Allan

AUTUMN

The grey clouds chase across the sky,
The rain falls to the earth,
The dry leaves say, 'Goodbye, goodbye,'
To trees they knew from birth.

And all around is silent - still.
Birdsong is seldom heard
Grey mist covers the distant hill
And muffles every word.

The countryside prepares to die
To live again next spring
When flowers in carpets glowing lie
And nesting songsters sing.

Then you and I will love again,
My darling, as before
And all the parting and the pain
Will be, please God, no more.

Mariann Walker

THE SEASONS OF THE MIND

When asked to define the seasons of the mind it's a difficult task
I'm wishing somehow I hadn't been asked

Spring brings to mind rebirth
A rising up of plants from the earth
The growing up of a child from babyhood
Just like the opening and blossoming of a brand new bud.

Summertime, everything's blooming, flowers, crops, hedges and trees
A time for outdoor activities or just sitting watching the birds and
the bees
We are now fully grown and at our best
Our minds and bodies are strong and full of zest.

Autumn is the time for the harvest being gathered in
As the saying goes, 'Free from sorrow, free from sin'
Hopefully a time for having reaped the rewards of our ambitions in life
Or having produced children, man and wife.

Wintertime is when Mother Nature takes her rest,
When winter storms put her stamina to the test
The main feature is retirement, of easing of the pace
So goes the saying, 'Grow old with grace'.

C D Kettle

WORDS FOR THE SEASONS

When spring is a joy
full of leaves to enchain her soft neck
its petals interblend to blossom her hair,
then dawn sky's morning colours her eyes.
Words now run with the lilt of her laughter
like rills skipping silver to cascade and sparkle
as ripples on a wind-dimpled stream.

Summer is joyful
mountains are peak blue at their summits;
her sheep now like mushrooms in buttons
farm collies bring down from green hills.
Words twist Titian curls to catch hay
in her hair loosely tumbling, before they soar
as a kestrel speeds to outrace, dive and plummet.

Autumn's joy is
sunlit leaves twisting and twirled, flying
as if birds encircle together making ready to leave
over deep swirls of sea, grey under their wings.
Words sweep with the inrush of rain over ploughed fields
drenching her hair like the mop from her bucket
saving her last gathered fruit from onsetting storms.

Winter is joy
washing freezes in shapes, line dried in crisp air;
her children race sledges to their freedom of snow
playing scarved brightly till supper and bed.
A peal of words rings to the night sky;
choirs sing joyfully vibrant with loved tunes
as her chapel holds carols high in its beams.

Dennis Marshall

WINTER JEWELS

Jewel like, the sky hangs
in varied layers of brilliant colours,
bands of sun-shot orange and yellow,
down near the horizon,
merging into cold blue above.
Black trees stand silhouetted against
the splendour of the heavens.
Bright brilliance presaging
bitter cold to come, this night -
sharp diamond studded sky,
sharp diamond studded ground,
and silent world in-between,
dark as jet or onyx,
hard as crystal,
cold cutting like a knife,
through the sapphire night,
waiting for the chilly hues
of the pearly dawn.

Anne Tompsett

DECEMBER

Early December
(Christmas panic setting in),
I'm kicking myself not to have done
More baking, more cleaning,
More shopping before now,
Power Rangers sold out,
No more Barbie Dolls,
And my 'taxi' is trying
to chauffeur them all
To the umpteenth carol service,
Traffic is going
Much too slowly,
I expect Bethlehem was as busy,
No room in the Inn.

M Boles

IN SPELLBOUND SEQUENCES

Seasons in their patterned play,
Passing spiritually away.
Rebirth spun from winter's chill
Inspires spring's awoken thrill.
Nervous buds prepare to burst,
Growth agog in air immersed.

Shimmering with sun-stroked shapes,
Undulations of landscapes
Move in maxim summer's spell,
Make waves for its miracle.
Effervescent textured lights
Rippling heydays of delights.

Autumn, awesome, coming soon.
Underneath its harvest moon,
Torn beyond the spectral sky,
Understands what has to die.
Mirrorings that solstice brings.
November's long-gone migrant wings.

Whither every withering
Inch of wizened wintering?
Nature's cruel compulsive death,
Tremendous as its aftermath;
Essence of vernal yearning
Remarkably returning.

David Coates

LANDSCAPE PAINTER

A scarlet evening,
Yesterday's leaving
To bring forth a brand new day,
The circle of life, once more, revealing
Mother Nature's time to play;
Ready to welcome in the dawn,
With a sunrise that is new,
Eclipse the fields of swaying corn,
Awash with a velvet dew.

The flowers greet the sun
With a heart open wide,
Their petals show a welcome mat
To the bees, to nip inside.
The animals who wake with the dawn,
Go about their daily chores,
As for me, I am the lucky one
I just sit and paint some more.

Curiosity's friend, the cat
Keeps a watching brief,
On movements that could endanger
The planets heart beneath,
A robin keeps an eye
Over this, his grand domain,
And I wonder if I
Will ever capture, a moment like this again.

Flowing water tells the Earth,
It never will run dry,
And the enriched soil will give birth,
To a fledgling infants cry;
Under shady pastures, lush and green
As blue sky colours the day,
Such a beautiful, majestic scene,
I never want to stray.

Paul Anthony Kearsey

THE VIEW

The view from our window is really fine
As I look out these thoughts are mine.
The fields and the brook are always there,
In the distance the farms, and neighbours we share.

In spring there's the flowers, with colours so gay
Children will gather them, to cheer up our day.
Little lambs with their mothers delightful to see
Running races and jumping as high as can be.

After a winter indoors, though bedded with straw,
The cows are all mooing to be out once more.
Now they're fighting and running and prancing around,
Delighted to feel their feet on the ground.

In eating the grass I know they will be,
Just filling their udders with milk for our tea.
Then summer is here with its warm sunny days
The grass growing tall for the mower to raze.

For haymaking too, it has to be done
And though it's hard work, there's still lots of fun.
The tractors are humming, from morning till night,
As they bring in the bales and pack them so tight.

In autumn the corn and potatoes too
Fruits are a-ripening to see winter through.
For winter it comes with its mantle of snow
Trees all a-glistening, the heaven's aglow.

Thus we move through the year, ever-changing the view
Till Christmas is here and another year too.

Dora Beswick

SUMMER EVENING IN STRESA

The waters of Maggiore lap lazily along
As on the promenade the evening strollers throng.
On distant hills shine bright fans of twinkling light
Contrasting with the violet shades of gentle night.

Beside the lake the visitors in twos and threes
In animated banter talk and walk at ease
And here and there, oblivious to the world around,
On starry nights in tight embrace are lovers found.

Children who by now should surely be asleep in bed
Hold parents' hands or, all excited, run ahead.
Observe how young and old are for the evening dressed;
Each girl in hope she's more attractive than the rest.

Across the way the road is lined with great hotels,
Whose chefs - some cordon bleu -weave gastronomic spells.
From hotel grounds sweet frangipani scents arise
As floodlit flowers lift sleepy petals to the skies.

Dark clouds are gathering as the last of daylight fades
And soon the rain streams down, torrential in cascades.
So straight it falls, a mere umbrella meets our needs,
And now bright hued they sprout like strange prolific weeds.

C Champneys Burnham

PASSING SEASONS

In spring we ran as children,
Through fields of palest green,
Climbing gorse-clad mountains,
The air was fresh and clean.

In summer we sat together,
Amid dunes of soft white sand,
And walked along the seashore
As lovers hand in hand.

In autumn we were married,
The leaves had turned to gold,
Our lives entwined forever,
What would the future hold?

Now snowy winter has arrived,
So many seasons passed,
The sceptics all confounded,
Said our love would never last.

I G Everett

IN HARMONY WITH THE SEASONS

I see the autumn trees aglow, with red and green and gold
I see the sky in blue and white, such colours I behold
Are shining through my dismal mood reminding me that never
Would there be such a gladsome glowing of the heath and heather
If first the rain of winter and then the summer sun
Had not maintained its well-planned course
Its allotted season's run
And so it is with us - every change is for our good
From babyhood through infancy - to man and womanhood
The sunshine of our starting as loved and cherished babes
The spring-like sprouting of our growth through awkward teenage stage
The worry of our middle years, we plod through winter weather
The autumn glow descends on us with quietness to mellow
And we look at our growing time and understand the reasons
Why our Creator made us all in harmony with the seasons.

Mary Howell

AUTUMN LEAVES

When the
Autumn
Leaves start
Falling
The birds stop
Calling
As they
Migrate
To warmer
Places
Then we will not
See their little
Faces
For a
While
And when
They finally
Return
Everyone can
Smile again

Coleen Bradshaw

MILLENNIUM DREAM

October sun precious as gold
  Riding low in the autumn sky
Shyly peeping through waving trees
  Shine for me as bleak winter draws nigh.

As golden leaves play in the breeze
  Birds migrate in the fading light
The trees will soon be sleeping too
  Long winter nights with their buds shut tight.

The days grow shorter and more cold
  Lost much too soon the warm sunshine
The seaside days we had this year
  Those summer gardens with grape-hung vine.

Crisp snow will cloak the hillside white
  Marauding foxes leave their tracks
We'll shiver in these draughty streets
  Folk in their thick coats or shabby macks.

When winter comes spring will follow
  Another millennium will dawn
I hope we live in times of peace
  As our brand new thousand years are born.

Fred Magan

SPELLBOUND

I was absolutely spellbound
  with the view confronting me
In a rainforest in Africa,
  thousands of feet above the sea.
The spot was called God's Window
  and one could understand why
As I'm sure we weren't far off Him
  as we'd seemed to climb so high.

Surrounding the forests were mountains
  -their peaks lightly shrouded in mist
Making a breathtaking scene for an artist
  - a landscape he couldn't resist.
Looking down on the valley below me
  was also an awesome sight
Where the tops of the trees formed a blanket
  of green which shimmered when touched by sunlight.

And away to my right where the trees weren't so
  dense, I could just glimpse the road that we'd used
As it twisted and turned going this way and that
  - like a snake that was out on a cruise.
Sadly our visit there came to an end
  as we had to continue our tour,
But if there's a Heaven for life after death
  - I've been there and seen it - for sure.

Joyce Crawford

SEASONS

A cheese-white moon fragmented on a troubled sea,
the wind blows fitful from Siberia
and penetrates our homes interior.
The bank refuses the money for a cup of tea,
they say that not even one more debit
may we add until we earn some credit.
And yet, in all of this, you choose to stay with me.

The full green leaves of willow dipping touch the Dee.
The late spring promises labour's return
if further labour we do not spurn.
The chance is here at last, we could run home free.
A little more of effort, time and drive;
just one more year and then we'll be alive.
And yet, in all of this, you choose to stay with me.

The apples hang, juice-heavy, on a groaning tree,
the sun shines through to dapple on your face,
at last there is some calm some sense of space.
Now there is the money needed for a spree.
We wine and dine and dance till after four
while knowing we can pay the piper's score.
And yet, in all of this, you choose to stay with me.

The northern wind blows chill from off the sea.
The garden takes again its winter shrouds,
as leaves a-stripped from branches in their clouds.
I limp, a martyr to arthritis in the knee,
and now each Friday there's the added chore
of queuing for my cash 'til half past four,
And yet, in all of this, you choose to stay with me.

David W Lankshear

CHRISTMAS AND THE MILLENNIUM

When I was young Christmas was at my grandmother's, the tree with
candles lit within the room.
A stranger dressed in red with beard and whiskers knocked on the door,
and led in from the gloom.
Sack in hand he walked towards the children singing carols all seated
on the floor.
The presents handed out were small but welcome, and Grandad
departed out of the door.

Next generation took upon the task and followed the tradition.
My mother and aunts, and uncles too would entertain.
Tables set with silver, glass, candles and best plates. A vacant place a
welcome just in case.
A dish placed in the centre, collected money for the poor. We all felt
very grateful that we could have much more.

In turn I tried to plan the Christmas party.
I cooked mince pies, turkey and ham, bread sauce and chestnuts too.
Spice added to the pudding, brandy-lit, crackers pulled with a bang, hats
put on round the table, to make happy was the plan.
We sang around the piano, played card games as of yore, we tried to
keep it merry as we had done before.

My daughters, sons and families invited us in turn.
We had to travel far from home to watch the coal fires burn.
Each year becomes more difficult to keep us all together.
So much depends on train or coach - it's harder in cold weather.

I think the sad part now I see - a fact I must accept
our family has split apart and none of them can get
to meet each other or to join in Christmas celebrations .
The family life that we once knew ends with this new millennium.

Doris E Pullen

THE WOODS IN MAY

When I walked out in the woods one day,
In the month of May,
In the woods one day in May.
When I walked out in the woods one day,
In the woods in the month of May

There were bluebells growing all around,
Growing on the ground
Growing all around the ground.
There were bluebells growing all around,
Pretty flowers everywhere abound.

There were blackbirds singing in the trees,
music on the breeze,
Singing on the breeze,
There were blackbirds singing in the trees,
Sweetest singing that to all doth please.

Nature's beauty, it was everywhere,
For us all to share,
Glowing for us all to share,
Nature's beauty it was everywhere,
Nature's beauty fresh and bright and fair.

Ken Jackson

WINTER

She says; 'Clouds are not always grey,
They are lilac and ochre
And a million other colours,
But you don't see it.
You don't see the beauty
Of rain on the river
Or hear in rhythmic drops
An eternity of hearts beating.
The fun of snowstorms,
Torn pillows of mock fights.
The bracing feeling of being alive.
The crumble sound of
Scuffing through dead leaves.
You are hedgehog-like,
Prickled by the changing weather -
You would hibernate winter away
Under a duvet
Not the colour of clouds.'

C Harris

A YEAR

The England we know and treasure
is steeped in a country rhapsody
sights and scenes in full measure
that portray
spring awash with dewy grass
and budding leaves
leaving behind the wood harsh strains
of winter, the crisp hard earth underfoot
boughs laden with snow
and robin dutifully watching behind the bough.
When suddenly spring bursts forth
the first daffodils appear
to awaken our souls with bliss
and summer is near
with roses in her hair, leaping with joy
as it unfolds, this is beauty at its best.
Thoughts of holidays and cricket on the green,
wickets falling, distant voices and things unseen,
And so to autumn a mellow feeling
of putting the past behind us
welcoming the sadness of bonfires
of woodsmoke and darkening days,
early morning mist
and the harvest gathered in.
Christmas at last, Christmas bells,
bright lights and heavenly things,
a year of thankfulness and we hold our breath
at the sound of oxen in the stall
to the wonder and magic of it all.

Joan Hands

AUTUMN

The dancer Autumn swings and sways,
flinging the cloak of colour
over the gardens, these short sunny days,
showing the best at last.
I cannot wait to gather gleaming sheaves,
to pile the baskets high with petalled flowers,
gold, scarlet, purple, orange, bronzing green.
Tomorrow blows the wind of Winter that bereaves,
tomorrow fall the soft destructive showers,
stripping away all colours that were seen,
until we say only a fool believes
the dancer Autumn tossed a rainbow cloak
then turned out Winter's lining - for a joke.

Ruth Partington

JOY

Another spring, another year.
Disappearing at last the fear
That we would not see the trees give leaf.
We would not see their blossom's brief
But glorious opening.
Not see the wondrous white
Against the blues.
Not see the greens of different hues.
Now finally we breathe again
Escaping from the winter's pain.
When darkness held us hostage.

Christine Clark

A Winter Storm

I am looking out, I am safe and warm,
Yes I am looking out, at the storm.
The thunder rolls, a mighty bang,
Then all is quiet, imagine if you can.

The lightning flashes, zigzags across the sea,
Angry waves battering the coast, you'll see.
The night is dark, the moon is hid,
To come from the clouds, the moon does bid.

No bird is heard, the night is still,
Except the rain, beating on the sill.
At last, a glimmer of sky is seen,
The storm at last, is now has been.

How many have stood here before,
Not knowing, what is in store.
I draw the curtains, I am safe and warm.
I was looking out, at the winter storm.

V M Foulger

THE FOUR SEASONS

Whenever I hear the blessings through the air
I know that the Lord God is everywhere
When we hear the voices of birds, sing so sweet
To know the good green earth, is underneath our feet

When blackbirds are heard with their songs of cheer
High alarms echo through the woodlands near
While, the mistle thrush listens, at early dawn
With a rasping chatter, as she sits on the lawn

When spring meets the summer, that is in view
The clouds unfold, turning the skies blue
Pure with the haze, the emerald sun dilates
The wings of the swallows come back to mate

Making their nests in old buildings disused
The sweet swallow's haunt, makes me feel quite amused
While, mother nature works again, through God's powerful Hand
Bringing out colourful flowers, that spread through out the land

When the summer meets the autumn, once again
The wind's whistle so boisterous, against the rain
While, the golden leaves are scattered on the ground
While trees stand bare, Mother Nature claims the wealth, around

Since the bracken turns yellowish, to gold
The fragrance of the autumn showers, seem so cold
Till, the morning sun gleams, to scatter the blazing flowers
Before the autumn meets the winter, reaching the dark hours

When the glooms of the mood's seasonable mist appears
To cloud the mysteries, as the beauty disappears
Until we hear the song thrush in the spring
When the seasons meet, that's how the good Lord brings

Jean P McGovern

SEASONS OF LIFE

People come and go like the seasons do
Forever changing, forever new
It's all a plan since time began,
And we all follow it seasons and man.

We start off like spring and learn to grow
And on to school to learn to know.
Then into summer when in our prime,
That's when we really start to shine.

Those autumn days when past our best,
We slow down and take a rest.
Then into winter at the end of life,
And we think of all the strife.

But mostly the good will outweigh the bad,
And as we look back we think how glad.
If we had not been part of it we would never know,
How the seasons come and the seasons go.

Robert Beach

THAT FIRST CHRISTMAS NIGHT

There is an air of wonder
And glory everywhere
As midnight herald a tiny babe
A child beyond compare.
See clear Jesus in the manger
Lord of all yet here he lies,
To the admiration of his loved mother
And the angels of the skies.
With his foster father quietly watchful
Also the animals in the straw;
And high above the shining star
That did the Magi draw.
And now dear children and -
Adults the wide world o'er
Your infant king adore,
And pay him loving homage
Like the shepherds did outpour.

Josephine Howe

WINTER'S COMING

November nights - grey dark begins to creep
Much sooner now, much closer to our door
When dusk, obscurely clad, arrives by four
And shadows, through the fading brickwork seep.
Then as we watch invading blackness sweep
Across the landscape - day exists no more
Leaves nothing but the hum within earth's core,
Whilst human kind sojourn and later sleep.

Then as secluded night slips into day
The stirring world awakes to shrinking light
Sprawled growth that's spent and turned to drab decay,
A sun whose rays are now no longer bright
Soft sleepy sinking autumn, almost gone,
Is making way for winter's sudden bite.

Jo Lewis

AUTUMN VIEWS

Autumn again,
Cold winds and rain,
The sun, red-dipped,
Low has slipped,
Now only sees
Leaf-bare trees,
Summer's ending,
Winter pending.

Light-laid gown
Of orange, brown
And yellow-gold,
The earth enfolds.
Tranquil days,
Mellow haze,
Fireside talks,
Or rustling walks
In leaf-deep lane.
Autumn again.

P W Pidgeon

SUMMER SCENES

Sunbeams dance upon the waves;
Golden sand envelops the shore;
Calm water laps around the caves;
Up above, the seagulls soar.

Gardens abound with colourful flowers;
Bees and butterflies are on the wing;
There's welcome shade in leafy bowers;
Joyfully the blackbirds sing.

Carpeted meadows fresh and green;
Scented blossom on the trees;
The air around so serene,
Not even the whisper of a breeze.

Grey country church with steeple high;
A retreat where one can pray,
And give thanks for the beauteous earth and sky,
Upon a glorious summer's day.

Bernice M Grocott

A NEW YEAR

This is not the time to begin a new year,
not when the land hunches and wears
the mist about its shoulders.

The day comes and goes and comes,
pendulums between half-drawn curtains,
too tired to shrug off tired indifference
or make an effort of hostility.

But somewhere else the sun persists,
and green spears pierce
the hard and frozen earth;
silent are those pangs of birth.

And we, we do not know
whether to leap or limp
or how to go forward, so
we venture one decisive foot
and drag the other one behind.

I pluck a picture from the past,
sustain suspended animation,
and keep a presence in the mind.

Marcia Ascott

WOODLAND MEMORIES

Squirrels roam gathering nuts,
Rabbits twitching as they play.
Pathways blanketed with leaves,
A hedgehog rolled up like a pin cushion.
I listen; the crunch and rustling leaves
Under the feet of creatures foraging.
The air so fresh upon my face,
Pungent smell of wild garlic, ferns and the
Perfume of bluebells.
Rough trees, sticky with sap, fungus,
Ladybirds gathering in a scarlet flash.
Treasured memories of woodland holidays.

Denise Arinze

SPRING ON THE LINCOLNSHIRE WOLDS

Spring is come; from winter's deep sleep
Earth awakes to new life.
Above our heads rises a lark
Filling the air with his song.
See, where the graceful spire of a church
Rises above the green-brown of the fields.
The trees all but burst into leaf,
Making a green haze on the horizon.

Look! primroses and celandine
Lift up their heads to the sun.
Green tips of corn pierce the furrow
All earth broken by new life.
New song, activity in every hedge
Reveals new secrets from day to day.
All this beauty! More yet to come!
Oh for eyes and ears alert
That none be missed.

Joan Francis

In Praise Of Spring

Spring is the season of a new life.
Designed to help us forget winter strife.
To urge us on, to help us cope.
The dawn of a new year of hope.
Cheered by the thought of summer soon to follow
Life takes on a new charge, banishes sorrow.
Summer follows quickly bringing more cheer
Days which are brighter, skies blue and clear
Time to reflect, to plan how to use
The freedom we have to go where we choose.
Time to work in our gardens or fields as may be
To prepare for the winter when we are not so free.
To count the many good things nature has provided
To store them in our minds, later to be divided
Along with the less cheery thoughts which will surely come
When the days are short and the weather glum.
This way we find our average to cover all the year
A thought to ponder when autumn time is here.
Autumn with its beautiful hues
Its hedgerows full of fruit and berries,
Between seasons it is hard to choose
There are so many ifs and buts and queries
But, be it not for spring which is the new start
There would be no summer or any other part.
We need to have a starting point for the seasons to go on.
We also need an end for spring to follow from.
All seasons have their reasons for being what they are
But to me, spring has always been the shining star.
The star which guides and shows the way through
To summer, autumn and winter which surely follow true.

R M Green

WINTER

The time switch now retracts one hour
and winter's red eyed signals glow
to mark the curtaining of night
with measured breaks of heat and light.

One earth obedient to solar power
One thousand summer skies so sweetly decked
                              but winter sour.
The aphelion solstice quickens night
to plunder northern latitudes of light.

Grey skies once faced a mushroom tower
and crushed the smile of every flower.
The sudden surge of white-hot light
brought fearsome lessons to day and night.

Frank Pittman

Two Certainties

Another year draws to a close
Leaving me apprehensive.
The future zigzags out before me
With no hint of what's to come.
Pitfalls lurk within the shadows
Holding many dangers, and
Each crossroad holds a different fate
With no one there to guide me.
In life, two certainties alone exist -
That the past is safe behind me,
Beyond the reach of change
And that death lies waiting for me,
Reaching out his hand.

Caroline Merrington

AUTUMNAL THOUGHTS

Autumn - the very word is like a knell,
The end of summer and its happy days
Of warmth and bounteousness amid the flowers
And fields of corn, and sun-warmed sweet by-ways.

But now the velvet golden nights of warmth
Are turning misty, chilly till the dawn,
The gentle days are filled with whirling leaves
And many are the apples on the lawn.

The sun sinks low and reddens in the west,
A glow that could not be a summer one,
The countryside is hushed, the wraithing mist
Steals o'er the fields and woods as day is done.

And in my heart a gentle sorrow falls
For all that's gone and is forever lost
As life winds down and days become as one,
Until we sing of Christ and snow and frost.

And then the joyous gladdening of the Soul
Carries me forward to the days of spring,
When lavish nature wakes and cuckoos call,
And sunshine warms and birds are on the wing.

Jenny Duckworth

SUMMER'S BOUNTY

Bees buzz from flower to flower
Among the poppies bright
Red against verdant summer's green.
Geraniums blue placid faces stare
As the busy morning rushes on its way to work.
Sunlight creeps from climbing clouds
As gentle breeze ripples
Leaf and flower.
Plump sparrow chirps, looking for food
Then flits to straw-strewn hutches
Where new life sleeps
In dreamy rabbit down, eyes just opening,
All cuddled up.
Busy mother pounds her door for food,
And yet more, to feed the hungry mouths.
Day lilies unfurl hesitantly,
Their beauty soon to fade
But traffic drones past
This quiet glade
Of my gardens, touched by summer's bounty
And soothes my soul before the day's hurtling strife,
The stillness captured in my heart.

Rosalind Duke

DAYDREAMS

Lying lazily among summer's gaudy flowers,
crushed by the weight of so many sunlit hours,
I sigh and gaze at busy ants among the blooms
and count the time till cooler months resume.
I crave cool water-colour autumn days,
russet fruits suspended in the haze,
as trees lay weary boughs to rest,
golden leaves by mists caressed.
I long for icy, wintry nights,
twinkling Christmas lights,
crisp white snow,
fires aglow.
I miss the spring, fresh new green,
reviving showers of crystal rain,
but these hot summer days are far too long and blue,
strange as that may seem to you.

Claire Ronxin

WINTER COMETH

Summer ends amidst the trees
Of turning multicoloured leaves,
Dressed in shades, red, brown and gold;
A sign the year is growing old.
Autumn's wind announces the cold,
For summer's warmth the world now grieves.

With ageing year must daylight fade,
In woodlands, leafy carpet newly laid,
Creatures hurrying, the year grows late,
Winter stores scurrying to create,
To survive the cold and hibernate.
A frosty silence falls on each forest glade.

The woodland waits in expectation,
Trees stand in naked, silent isolation,
Against winter frosts, snows and chills.
Stoically suffering the seasonal ills,
As winds invade from northern hills
Bringing winter's beautiful desolation.

Bry Lingard

SPACES

Out of doors and over moors
the ripple wind in hair.
With striding step and racing heart
we stream the bracing air -

And clear our minds of jagged saws
at bouncing heather tread
are lifted, urged into the fresh
and wide expanse ahead -

We stretch our limbs and lunge for space
our minds all blown and free
before the vastness that enfolds
of mauve and sky and sea -

How small our sights and petty views
now seem beside this scene
where multicolours, beauty, peace
speak realms of mystery -

What wondrous power has fashioned them
what hand of majesty
that awe-inspires and humbles us
yet thrills and sets us free?

Rosemary Keith

A RHYME FOR WINTER

The snow lies thick upon the ground,
It falls to earth with ne'er a sound.
The shepherd blows upon his nail
The ice lies thick within the pail.

The cheeky robin cocks his head
Prickly hedgehog goes to bed.
Trees stripped bare of all their leaves
Cruel winter has no thought for these!

Frost covers every hip and haw,
Icicles hang from the stable door.
Wily old fox heads home to his den -
He's been raiding the chicken pen.

Christmas cards hang from the chimney wall,
Wreaths of holly deck the hall.
Berries of mistletoe, smooth as a pearl
Are a welcome sight for each boy and girl.

Logs on the fire, flames burning bright,
Keep out the cold of the oncoming night.
Church bells ring out, so loud and so clear
Welcoming in a brand New Year.

Patricia Whiting

THE WAY OF THINGS . . . PASTORAL

Birds over the fen fly to height
Languid with masterful wings
Trees by the lakeside soar to height
Limbs stirring gently
Over the lake small ripples spread
Mirroring the mirror of the world
Men on the road leave and clamber the bank
There to relax
In the ambience of the day
As the leaves turn to the sun
As the birds head for home . . .

Michael C Soper

PURPLE NOVEMBER

Purple November,
Far to the east;
Pink every ember,
Yellow like yeast
Sun on the river,
Rays almost ceased,
Gilt on each cluster,
Autumn deceased,
Light almost over,
Hills to the south,
Darkness will hover,
The wide valley's mouth;
Sky looking greyer,
Drawing a close,
Green and magnolia;
Delicate rose.

Tom Ritchie

FUCHSIA

Last summer
In your flaming redness
I plucked you from your branch
Pressed you into darkness
Autumn you saw the light
Silver-framed on my mantelpiece
You bring summer
To my winter . . .

Margaret Toppin

TO SUMMERTIME

Summertime . . .
A time for walking by a stream.
To find a little shady nook
And quietly sit and dream.
To take a hike or ride a bike.
To wander through a wood.
To tramp across the open fields
The warm sun feeling good.

On sunny days to ramble,
Pick blackberries from the bramble.
To run happily through a meadow
With arms stretched to the sky.
To amble by a river,
And watch the little ducks swim by.
To stroll along a country lane.
To look at the view from a hilltop high.

Elaine Cooper

THE DARK NIGHTS AND WINTER

The dark nights I hate, the winter seems so long.
And I wonder where on earth do I belong!
My children have grown up, my husband's no more,
I feel so broken, right down to the core.

O where can I turn to, and with whom can I talk?
I'm tired of being shut in, and everything's so dark.
I start to pray, O Jesus, will you listen to my cry?
He says *I'm listening to you, and I long to satisfy.*

And then I look around me, all that I have I see,
O thank you Lord, O thank you for drawing close to me.
For my home and all its warmth, for food and for rest.
I know the plans you have for me, are indeed the best.

The darkness now is lifting, I say thank you Lord for this,
For as I go to bed tonight, I know I'll sleep with bliss.
And tomorrow when I wake up, you'll be there by my side,
I'll be able to pray for others, for in you I can confide.

Doreen Beckingham

THE FOUR SEASONS

Spring . . .

Springtime flowers so colourful in bloom
Springtime sunshine lights up the darkest room
Springtime sights and sound to lift the gloom
Springtime scent and fragrance a lovely perfume

Summer . . .

The soft summer breeze so gently does blow
And the warm summer sun brightly does glow
And lovely coloured flowers in our gardens grow
As trees full of blossom give a magic summer show

Autumn . . .

The autumn hues and colours are spread everywhere
Autumn trees without leaves stand stark and bare
Autumns pale sunshine so brightly does glare
As the autumn leaves are blown around here and there

Winter . . .

Winter frosts so crisp and bitterly cold
Winter winds so blustery fierce and bold
Winter snow so white has taken its hold
Winter mist and fog their dampness unfold

Anthony Carlin

ENGLISH WEATHER!

January starts a brand new year, with all its untouched days,
We make some resolutions for improving our bad ways.
February continues cold, there's snow and ice about.
The roads are very dangerous, so we do not venture out.
March blows in but when it's here, the birds begin to sing.
We hope the weather brightens up, as soon it will be spring.
April brings its showers, but we welcome spots of rain,
For once they stop, we don't wait long to see the sun again.
May's the month with lots of change, so hot and yet so cool,
But often quite delightful, we enjoy it, as a rule.
June - the month of long hot days, and evenings staying lighter.
July we get some thunderstorms, but weather soon gets brighter.
August sometimes can be hot, we've now acquired our tan,
We make the most of sunshine, staying outdoors when we can.
September brings the autumn, when the colours start to change,
For nature does her party piece, to show us such a range.
October's Indian summer, you'll not hear us complain,
It helps to shorten winter, when the cold is here again.
November days are very short, don't get a glimpse of sun.
It's mostly damp and cold and mist, November's not much fun.
December days are shorter still, the light is very poor,
But folk don't mind, it's Christmas soon, the time they're waiting for.
With Christmas over, people cheer . . .
We soon will start another year.

Doris Gallard

THE RETREAT

A country cottage 'reserved' to stay.
The perfect place for a hide-away.
In solitude - a peaceful start,
For calm repose to allay the heart.

Pile on the logs for wood-burning stove,
An old fashioned range in a quaint alcove.
Cajoling bright flames of orange to stoke
Which sparks and crackles with every poke.

Settled in niche - all snug and cosy.
Blushing features soon appear rosy.
And in the firelight's magical beam.
Imagined pictures softly gleam.

Ready for sleep with nodding head.
Tread the creaking stairs to bed.
With feather pillows and crisp white sheets,
Safely wrapped in slumbering deeps.

Eagerly rise with the morning sun,
To explore the country scenes have come.
By verge and hedgerow fuchsias bloom,
In their season - wild cherries and broom.

These halcyon days that refresh the senses.
Are far from modern influences.
To witness the bounty in nature's parade,
A charmed spectator would not trade.

With nature's blessing comes a mantle of calm.
Restored in essence - a soothing balm.
Departing at last with wistful glance,
Thinking - I'll come again. . . perchance!

Joy M Jordan

PENSIVE IN FEBRUARY

On a weathered fence
a sunless robin flutters,
February day.
On a withered branch
a moonlit owl settles down,
February night.
In my window box,
silk-white snowdrops tell me they
were there all the time.
Along the old fence
brittle vines shiver, whisper
they will soon be mine.
In frozen clay pots
spiky white hyacinths strive
to keep their promise.
Peeping through old leaves
yellow primroses remind
me of sun-felt days.
And on the old gate,
with the broken latch hanging,
honeysuckle clings . . .

Maureen Bold

Autumnal

When late summer fades into autumn
And ripening hedgerow fruits are awesome.
Nodding bluebells are in open glades,
With bright yellow bracken in the shade.
Shrilling of grasshoppers in the air
Wasps and jam sandwiches are the fare.
And the rays of the sun warm the soil
While nests of black garden ants do toil,
Then they swarm in the air, where they mate.
Wheat is combined for the harvest fete.

On water lilies, perch damsel flies.
And charms of gold finches perch nearby.
Curlews probe the mud with their long beaks;
Flicking pebbles beside meadowsweet.
In the fields tiny harvest mice hide
Among brambles, they breed and abide.
Skipper butterflies search for nectar
Around platinum lakes, what a spectre!
Pine trees stand against a moonlit sky.
Ghostly shadows tell evening is nigh.

Ann Easton

A WINTER SCENE

The spring, the summer and the autumn have passed,
Now winter is here, with ice and cold blasts.
I see from my window, the frost on the lawn,
The leaves have fallen, from the hedges of thorn.

But midst the bare branches, of the bushes and trees,
Sit the birds of our gardens, in the cold chilly breeze.
Each winter they come, from the meadow and field,
Using our gardens, and walls for a shield.

You look for their colours, as they puff out a chest,
There always amongst them, is robin red-breast.
Blue tits and coal tits and sparrows galore,
Great tits and chaffinch, and so many more.

Their coming confirms now, that winter is here,
But their presence amongst us, fills you with cheer.
You can put out some nuts, and crumbs on the lawn,
And feed them each day, at the coming of dawn.

It's a pleasure to look on the antics they play,
When they take a small crumb, then up and away.
A few moments later, some more they will seek,
And carry away, holding tight in the beak.

Then comes the day, when you see the snow fall,
You build them a table, and set for them all.
It's nice to relax then, to enjoy each new day,
You know through the winter, your bird friends will stay.

Donald Futer

SILENT SPRINGS

The swans are back again
Nesting upon the island in the lake.
Each year in early spring
Returning to the scene of last year's nuptials.
And last year's young are gone now:
We watched them as they grew, grey down turning
To beige and, finally,
To dazzling white upon the water.
Now they return, once more
Building their nest, the dam already broody,
Framed by the bushes, leaves as yet unfurled.
Her mate circles the island
Chasing away the geese, skimming
Across the surface of the water.

Each year it tears my heart,
Remembering - we too once built a nest.
Our young have gone and we
Return no more.
Only the ghosts of half-forgotten springtimes
Now haunt our ancient memories.

Dorothy Davis-Sellick

SUNNY AFTERNOON

Hot sun, eased by a gentle scented halcyon breeze
Blue sky, sparsely speckled with slow drifting cloud
Textbooks, untouched, abandoned to count butterflies
Mind languishing, serene, dreamlike, all senses at rest
Unsilent silence, interrupted by the harmonious busy bee
Sleepy eyes, alerted momentarily to the soaring acrobatic swallow
Birdsong, gathering momentum, signalling the advent of dusk
Chilling air, prising mind and body from their subtle seducer
Stretching, yawning, as day surrenders to night's velvet cloak
Essay unfinished, whilst communing with nature, digressing in style.

Elizabeth Skidmore

SUMMER

Such disappointment, little buckets, spades and waders
Clutter the holiday cottage grass
While plastic-macked and welly-booted
The youngest youngsters trail the cold grey sand.

The sea and sky an endless damp diffuseness
Sounds flattened, gulls evaporate, to where?
Wavelets sigh and plop as show sad tears
Strands of seaweed parody Medusa's hair.

We'll go a walk else the day seems longer
The day is very long and wet and sulks
Bright bathing towels dry the rain-soaked hair
A coaxed fire crackles up the chimney, oh sweet heat.

Bless the morrow, it's blustery, blue and golden
Was ever grey invented? Look, islands just offshore.
With joy the boat is lifted from the trailer
Mum, can we do everything at once?
Yes! Yes! Now summer's here.

Vie Tulloch

FOUR SEASONS

Pale shafts of sunlight will filter thro' trees
To the crocus who opens her eyes and sees
The soft fluffy clouds in the pale blue sky
A bird who is voicing an echoing cry
This is the season when all things awake
When wise Mother Nature surveys hill and lake.

Roses are heavy and full-blown on stem
The delicate perfume that's wafted from them
Is borne on the lazy hot summer air
To the stream as it ripples past meadows so fair
This is the season of hoe and of rake
Straw hats and picnics and boats on the lake.

Trees gently sway and their leaves flutter down
Spreading their carpets of amber and brown
Creating a sad sense of loss and decay
A wistful reflection, they've outlived their stay
This is the season of rust and of gold
The time when we realise that all things grow old.

The sky is grey and overcast
The wind bursts in with icy blast
Bearing a gift he'll so roughly bestow
The first soft and gentle flurry of snow
This is the season that Jack Frost will freeze
The time of the snowman, the cough and the sneeze.

The crispness of winter, the warm breath of spring
The mellowness of autumn, summer's bird on the wing
Thus all of the seasons with their own special charms
Will each take their turn, as with wide open arms.
They greet the warm earth so receptive and kind
And leave yet another long year behind.

Alma Annette Sewell

SEASONS

With what certainty the seasons change,
Early on one see only grass,
And then the snowdrop appears
With the crocus and the daffodil.

These grow beneath the cherry blossom
To announce the spring in silent beauty,
And careless of their loveliness
Wait for the timely death.

This happens and bluebells cover the grass,
Yet these flowers only last
Till the canopy thickens
And shadows the self-same ground.

The later flowers both wild and cultivated
Grow in abundance, yet never untimely
They die too when summer ends
And the year matures.

Yet even here there is a beauty
As leaves alter and fall,
And snow descends to cling
And drift awesome in its power.

Never untimely the seasons change,
Altering the temporal state of things,
Knowing yearly what each one brings,
There is nothing more certain than this.

Robert William Lockett

AUTUMN IS . . .

The reddish glow
Of apples, promising sweetness -
And stomach ache, laying a scrumper low.

Autumn is . . . the end of lemonade
And outdoor-cafe summer. Folk
Walk less along the esplanade.

Autumn is . . . trees trying on
New uniforms, and mounting guard
Of honour over roads I ride along.

Gillian Fisher

THIS AUTUMN

Fires stand in the evening skies
Dropping sparks on holly trees.
Blue skies laze across the mornings
Silting up fogs and frosts.
Leave fall capriciously
Brown ashes gold on red.
The blues and pinks
Of summer's last flowers
Flaunt unseasonable colours.
Blackberries burn
While apples tumble
Shaken profusely from
Overburdened trees.
And the sun fights boldly
Fending off white rime
And darkening days.

Sylvia Goodman

WINTER

Autumn glory makes way for winter,
Days of cold and damp.
Cheery fires and crumpets for tea.
Take a walk down a winding lane,
Listen to the stillness,
See in the hedgerow the forgotten berry,
Once again the circle has gone round.

Overhead the sky is dark,
The great oak throws wide its arms,
To shelter the animals and birds,
That not so long ago played thro' its leaves.
Now those leaves, that were once so green,
Are lying brown and wrinkled beneath our feet.

Half remembered childhood as we wander
Through the woods -
Collecting chestnuts and the most favourite
Of mine, the shiny brown conker!
Winter's delights are there for young and old,
But some have dimmed with time.

Holly and ivy trailing down,
Collecting logs and kindling,
To burn a fire to sit around -
'Look at those pictures!'
The flickering flames grow and dim,
To a dying ember -
Then it's the end of December!

Aileen Andrews

SUNDAY

The road one day at Easter
Light and shade divided.
A side for spring and winter;
Celandines glowed; were frosted.
Differing beauty, for,
On some the sun shone;
The others had none.
Tho' this changed as the day went on.

Maxine Bracher

NATURE

A field full of dancing golden corn,
The first rays of light herald a bright new dawn.
The far-off sounds of innocent laughter,
Sparks off another day,
Of little children busy at play.
A gentle breeze glides autumn's first gold leaves.
Poppy heads dance around,
Scattering seeds upon the ground.
Lilac and lavender perfume the air,
Into a world full of love and care.
A hedge full of bright berries for birds to eat,
When winter comes calling at their feet.
The scuttling of a fieldmouse can be heard,
The suddenness of a startled bird.
All of this is nature in all her splendour,
To keep so wild and free and tender.

Sally Hunter

Colours Of Autumn

Golden and brown, tumbling down, leaves from their branches now fall.
Scarlet from green, lighting the scene, a paintbox of colours for all.
Orange and red, bright overhead, as sunlight bright sparkles on dew,
river reflection a rainbow of light, the sky a wide backcloth of blue.

Bark tinted gold by the rays of the sun, tree branches sway in the light,
swirling and sweeping the leaves scatter down, while hands tug the
strings of a kite. All round the common the trees fill the dawn, with
orange, fine gold and sad green, scarlet and amber, yellow and brown,
lending new tints to the scene.

Summer is gone now, its days are far flown, lush greenery tired and
wan. Home from the park are the children who played, while the clock
in the hall marches on. Darkness falls swiftly now and night descends,
all glittering after the day, so treasure these weeks and the beauty they
bring, their colours will soon pass away.

Richard Langford

WINTER

The heavy snows of winter have just begun to fall
As Arctic conditions sweep in, surprising us all
I glance out across the garden at the everchanging scene
The lawn, a carpet of white which was once a shade of green.

I spot a solitary robin as he makes his way;
Along the hedgerow, on this winter's day
A thrush leaves footprints on the virgin snow;
As he forages for a grub or worm, his head down low.

It eases; I wrap up warmly and wander down to the park,
Where warmly clad children play, dogs they do bark,
I think back to my childhood, oh what fun I had,
Tobogganing down the hill, a fresh-faced lad.

The cold winds are biting, I shiver and turn,
I love the fresh air, but the warmth I do yearn
I walk up my path and then turn the key,
I settle down by the fire, just my memories and me.

Maggy Copeland

AUTUMN AND WINTER

Autumn coloured leaves coming off the trees, wind whistling,
                                        blowing them around,
It picks them up for another look before they reach the ground.
You can't creep about, without the sound of crunching under shoes,
Animals alert and hiding their eyes to see all your moves.
I like the sounds of autumn, leaves fluttering on their way down,
The squirrels busy scurrying, before the winter lays its white gown.
Autumn sun is colder now, the heat's gone out of the day,
Animals seem to change over, some tuck themselves away.
Trees are bare, it's late autumn, cold weather about to begin,
Birds of prey are watchful, as hunger starts to set in.
Atmosphere is changing, sharp frost is now forecast,
Plus gale force winds come over, give off their icy blast.
A flurry of snow is falling, snowflakes on windowpanes,
Snowmen are in the making, it's time for the wintry games.
Exposed now, into winter's advances,
Snow balancing on the twigs and branches.
The white carpet of splendour is thawing,
Next season about to be calling.
These are the things that I can see,
It's what autumn and winter mean to me.

Beverley Diana Burcham

DELAYED DEPARTURE

Still here, and singing, you little crazy bird?
It's not summer now you know, it's fall;
It's time your song in other climes was heard;
You shouldn't hang around at all.

I hope you've had a most successful year
And all your young are safely on their way
And may I say you're always welcome here
To sing your song some future summer's day.

But now the nights are drawing in,
The sun sinks lower in the sky;
The trees are looking bare and thin
As windswept leaves go scurrying by.

So bon voyage, head south, you lucky bird
While I remain to face the winter snow.
I wish I too had wings just like a bird,
We'd quickly find a warmer place to go.

G S Baker

OF, AUTUMN

It's just the weather
Taking me
Down
Memory lane

With autumn
Creeping in

The coldness

As I lie on my bed
Not wanting to get out of
The covers

Not wanting to go
Where I need to
Be

At my
Therapy

After the
Summer break.

Memories of
Having to go back to
School

Back to learning

Being
The child.

I can almost
See
The reds, oranges, browns
Dead leaves
On the trees

Of, autumn . . .

Paula Walsh

A Brief Respite

Riding my chemicals,
between apathy and all's well,
one still night,
my good eye saw a mackerel sky.
Aerodynamically rare.
I tried to think of its Latin name,
but we didn't go that far.

Around me, look,
just for one minute, please,
don't ask me to do anything.
I can't alter the amount of good,
that wraps around me.
Why consider its merits?
Why compare it to a thunderstorm
or a daffodil
on the A591?
It's nearly gone.

It's only nature's waste patterning high.
That sometimes dumbfounds the wise.
Only stupid me who lives a lie.
Needing solace from a mackerel sky.

I turn down and around.
A little loving gesture that still curtails freedom.
The cigarette turns tail.
And with it,
my fifteen minutes of stardom.

Mike Parker

BEAUTIFUL CREATION

Have trees always been beautiful,
In summer, winter and spring?
Did autumn always hold such tranquillity,
Since the start of nature's begin?

Spring has such pretty affection,
And brings with it nature's sweet bloom,
And softens the day with the blossom,
While taking away winter's cold gloom.

Summer's the season for flowering,
And the buds of love nest in the air,
And the leaves of the trees slowly increase,
Under the sun's blazing care.

In autumn the leaves all turn golden,
Orange, yellow, brown too,
And dance to the ground before winter,
Following nature's set rule.

Winter shows the tree naked,
Baring its limbs all askew,
With gnarled branches all twisted,
This nature knows to be true.

Suzanne Nicholls

MY GARDEN IN WINTER

The summer has passed, my garden looks bare
It's taking a rest from the cold damp air
Fog, ice and frost, just means one thing
It's a long dreary wait until the spring.
Old winter's arrived with winds and snow
Mysterious shapes now start to show.
Gusty winds take flakes to flight
Making ghostly figures dressed in white.
Snowflakes falling without a sound
How pretty they look, as they swirl around.
A lovely white blanket to keep the earth warm,
helping the roots and bulbs to form
Now wild birds stop by for food
That keeps me in a cheerful mood,
Chatting and chirping and making a fuss
The food is good, and the carpet plush,
These birds don't seem to mind at all
They know my garden, wall to wall.
It's like a party, a real treat
When they drop in for a bite to eat.
Now the frosty icing on the trees
Making wintry pictures just to please.
And sure enough it makes my day
It's a shame to see it melt away.

D Groom

AUTUMN

As I gaze upon the tree outside my humble home
I notice the inevitable change of the season that has come
In months gone by it flourished, although a brief affair
For now the garden tree is completely bare
Scattered round the base lie the leaves crisp and brown
Like bodies on a battlefield torn mercilessly down
It does appear a tragic time as autumn is now here
This only means one thing to me, winter is near.

Paul Christopher Holland

THE ICE AGE

Into a glass the young man stared
and saw the world grow old
before his very eyes the sun
had suddenly grown cold

A darkness greater than the night
plunged everything in gloom
and bitter cold came creeping in
the once familiar room

He looked again and dimly saw
the ocean's crumbled bed
littered with a million wrecks
on which the urchins fed

Become a snow white blanket now
as flakes began to fall
they settled on the broken earth
a shroud to cover all

Through the mist of frozen white
the young man saw no sign
of living creatures on the earth
there was no trace or kind

The grip of ice had strangled
all that lived and grew
and brought the silence of the grave
to a world that never knew

The young man slowly turned away
so troubled was his soul
as he beheld an ice-cold world
begin to spin and roll

Free of its orbit chains at last
it sped into the night
onto its own destruction
a brilliant flash of light

R G Stevens

FALLING LEAVES

I love to hear the leaves
Rustling through the trees,
And hear them crisp and crunch
Whilst walking through my lunch.
That first leaf brings autumn
Leaving the trees solemn,
Bereft, bare, naked
Until they're frost coated.

K Axon

Autumn Spirit

The summer has gone and autumn is in the air,
The days are shorter, the nights are longer,
For every season there is a reason,
The cycle rotates as nature intended.

Now is the time for trees to drop their leaves,
But before the final fall,
The hues of the leaves from green and gold through amber and red,
Are like wine to the senses.

Reflected in lochs and lakes,
Their image, a bonus, for artists found in unexpected places
In their endeavour to transpose the tapestry of colours on to paper,
A memory to keep and to brighten the day,
An effort to delay the onset of winter.

So, before it is too late,
You should make a date,
To walk in the country
And see the autumn bounty.

The trees in all their changing glory,
The copper beech, the Virginia creeper in deepest red,
Contrast with the yellowing of the oak
And the green of the evergreen.

Enriching the soul, as the soil is enriched by the leaves,
Providing everlasting memories and showing as the seasons pass,
That in death there is new life lurking,
Just waiting for spring to be released.

Mary Lawson

AUTUMN SCENE

Painted skies of red pink and yellow
Autumn sunset reflected so mellow
Heaven's embers viewed from Earth
Sun burning radiantly in her hearth
Lighting up the vibrant atmosphere
Combined adjacent forever adhere
Trees undressing shedding leaves of gold
Flowers dying with dignity in the cold
Nature's way of saying a sombre goodbye
Some survive while most plants die

Corn in meadows left lying in bales
Heather withering in hills and vales
Rust-coloured bushes turning to golden shades
Meandering mosses surviving in craggy glades
Bracken crackling briskly in shabby woods
Brooms lost blooms exuberant in various moods
Wildlife searching and striving for winter supplies
With zeal and vigour each one logically applies

Ann Copland

HAPPINESS

To hear the birds so joyfully sing
And see the butterfly on the wing
Or yet watch buds burst forth in spring
Makes me happy.
When close-shorn sheep jump hedges high
Or startled rabbit hurtles by
And trees in summer breezes sigh
I'm happy.
When autumn leaves of gold and brown
Softly cover woodland ground
As birds migrate from all around
I can be happy.
If fog enshrouds the countryside
Or snowflakes blanket far and wide
While wintry winds howl by outside
Still I'm happy.
For soon the birds will once more sing
And I'll see butterflies on the wing
Then watch the buds burst forth in spring
Content and happy.

L Summers

FIELDS OF ARDEN

Sitting in the fields of Arden,
we watch the jealous sky.
Sitting in the fields of Arden,
scared horses gallop by.

Sitting in the fields of Arden,
asking the gay sun to shine.
Sitting in the fields of Arden,
listening to the sad wind whine.

Sitting in the fields of Arden,
with an emotional content.
Sitting in the fields of Arden,
With the dreams you can only rent.

Jamie Barnes

AUTUMN

Crowded last gasps
in a cellophane sky.
Brittle brilliance and
brief magnificence,
engulf summer's tree
with fool's gold.

Laden with
shimmering ripeness
and fat seeds,
pallets of melting shades
decorate perfect posture -
nature's proudest piece.

But glory stirs deep unease.
Opulence misguides,
canopies are deliberately thinned,
golden warm tears are shed -
rusty red death mask
signalling another year's end.

And as I shiver
with a desolate above
and decaying below,
leaf after leaf fall,
and shake me aware
of the feebleness of my all.

Timothy Fisher

PATTERN

The leafy green, the verdant scene,
Where Nature is mild and mellow;
Until autumn imposes its own russet glories,
To alter the effervescent gleam
Then, life becomes sombre, the darkness gets longer
Winter finally phases out the incandescent beam;
Yet the ice and the snow give a comforting glow
To they who enjoy scenic extreme, then,
When spring once again bursts into bloom
Nature's rotational cycle does resume.

Renée Duckworth

AUTUMN

And skeletons of leaves blanket the ground,
And swirling winds sharp and shrill.
And old dead bracken trodden down,
And chattering birds that start and trill.
And clattering of milk-cans, whirling fog,
And coloured scarves wrapped warm and tight.
And flickering fires, thick, grey smog
And badgers snuffle through the night.
And echoes of footsteps stomping by,
And rain that falls into puddles that slosh,
And mugs of steaming chocolate.

And autumn skies, deep scarlet and brown,
And dark nights that creak with night sounds.
And dark nights that creak with night sounds.

Stephanie Harris

WINTER DIET

The cow stops chewing,
pauses,
leans against the byre wall
to think.

This can't be right
she muses
and yawns,
fogging the air.

She scrapes a hoof
on damp straw,
turns her head.
Big eye searching.

I am cow.
I amble through green fields.
I am white patched on black
like moonlit clouds on night sky.

I lie down in rain.
I moo, I bellow,
I shy away from dogs,
I eat grass.

In the summer
I herd outside.
In the winter
I steam in the byre.

Stabled between
441 and 132,
we sway and chew
until the spring.

But if this is what we are
- cow -
why are we fed sand eels?
And who will feed the seabirds
when they start to starve?

Matilda Webb

IN A SPRING BEECHWOOD

Like pale green lace
Anchored to earth
By black.

Sun filtering through
This delicate
Tracery.

We walked beneath
On velvet soft
Green plant.

A tangible whisper
Surrounded all
With peace.

Pat Rees

THE ENGLISH SEASONS

The seasons are like friends;
Each one different in its own way.
They flow into one another like a swirling river,
Although they couldn't be more separate, than night or day.

Spring arrives like a jack-in-the-box,
There is no doubt about when it is time
For the chicks to start hatching and the flowers to bud,
For every living thing to be in its prime.

Then comes the summer, to ripen the fruit,
And to allow the lambs to prepare.
For the winter is coming, and soon will be here,
To freeze everything from tree to hare.

The autumn follows close behind,
To decay the rich green leaves.
To lower the temperature and strengthen the wind.
That soon it will be winter I cannot believe.

And now winter itself is here once more,
To put the world at rest.
I don't know, I cannot be sure,
Which season I love best.

Brigitte Gebhardt

WHEN AUTUMN COMES

At first we hardly know that autumn's coming
The days are warm still, and the evenings long
But suddenly the trees are ripe-fruit laden
And we hear no more the nightingale's sweet song

And then the woods begin the autumn changes
At first a tinge, and then a gradual spread
Of colour, until all around an ocean
In shades of orange, russet, silver, gold and red

Too short, too short a time this autumn wonder
Too soon the rain and gales and early frost
The tortured branches cannot hold their treasure
The transient beauty once again is lost

The leaves in all their various shades of colour
From palest silver to rich russet brown
Glisten and shine in golden autumn sunlight
And dance and twirl as they come tumbling down

So for a while the scene is dark and sombre
Stark branches black against grey leaden sky
All life suspended as the woodlands slumber
And the damp, dull, dreary days pass slowly by

But very soon another change awaits us
When we awake, the world is shining white
Like diamonds in a shining sea of silver
The hoar frost has transformed the sorry sight

Migrating ducks and geese and swans returning
From frozen northern lands now reappear
And then we know the dismal days are over
Autumn has gone, and wintertime is here.

Estelle James

OCTOBER SONG

Low are the clouds, and from the sea
The mist is rising to meet the sky.
Leaves slowly falling from ev'ry tree.
Migrating birds don't sing, but cry.

The fields are bare, the harvest in,
The golden grapes are full of promise.
Between branches, busy spiders spin.
Dewdrops - jewels through the sun's kiss.

Storm winds are blowing round the house.
High tides are battering all our shores.
Such autumn weather finds man and mouse
Safely and warmly curled up indoors.

October - harvest - autumn time,
Long winter ev'nings will soon be here.
High raise your glasses, full of young wine,
Looking ahead to Christmas cheer.

Helga Dharmpaul

NATURE'S EVENTIDE ART

Fascinating streaks of colour
strike vividly through whispering leaves
then rebound onto quaking grass tops
creating carpets of a Persian theme
this bounteous act of nature
presenting art each eventide
displays in sunset glory
the hour is near for solitude
reminding all with visual splendour
that as day dies deep night awakes
and in its dark complacency
emits a halo of brilliant stars

H A Brawn-Meek

SUMMER

I love the early mornings
When everything's so still
Just the ticking of the clock
Birds singing a soft shrill
A breeze is gently blowing
Through the trees outside my house,
Everyone's asleep.
quiet do not rouse
The only signs of life are the early
Paper boys,
Even they are half asleep
They hardly make a noise
There is new dew in the garden
Which makes the grass look fresh
It's a lovely summer morning
Warm and clear not nesh.

Christa Fisher

MAY

May is such a glorious month, I wish it stayed for ever
Lilac blooming everywhere, and birds all sing together
The seeds upon the sycamore, laburnum blooming yellow
Tall irises with heads of blue, aubretia waxing mellow
Pansies mass with human faces, wallflowers waft their scent
How I love these simple pleasures laced with sentiment
All around the trees are green, their branches thick with leaves
The magpie and his mate are there, as in and out they weave
If twenty months were in the year, I still would proudly say
Give me the one that stands supreme, the merry month of May.

Betty Shenton

AUTUMN'S PATCHWORK

See the deep golden hues and soft burnished browns
Throughout the countryside and all around the towns
Greens, yellows and russets of every hue and shade
All things heaven-sent and definitely not man-made
Still cold waters mirror sharp images on a clear frosty morn
A lone rosebud on the briar hangs crisp and quite forlorn
Tendrils of mist streak the landscape as the rime softens to dew
Gossamer threads fill the air as the sun rises up fresh and new
Cascades of multi-coloured leaves fall gently from the nodding trees
Drifting and sighing, fluttering and flying all ruffled by the breeze
Conkers have fallen, sweet chestnuts for the fire are just right
And children of all ages find nature's toys a sheer delight
The hedgehog curls his body tight and rolls up in the leaves to sleep
And squirrels bury their store of nuts the winter for to keep
Put out bread and peanuts now, give our feathered friends a treat
While poor Reynard scrubs below the mulch for tasty grubs to eat
Natural treasures bedeck the woodland floor all colours on display
Fly Agaric, King Arthur' Cakes and Fairy Clubs on stumps hold sway
The hedgerow's hung with glorious jewels of berries, hips and haws
Rooks congregate round treetop roosts with raucous cries and caws
And holly densely green and glossy while teasels tall and stark
Stand out against a brassy sunset ebbing into autumn's dusty dark

Jean Selmes